Adventures of a Civil Servant

Jim Mackley

By the same Author

A Child in Paradise?: Wymeswold 1939–1958

I Went There on my Bike: The University Years

Copyright © 2021 Jim Mackley

New edition © 2024

All rights reserved.

ISBN-13: 9781917130226

For Jennifer

who let me do all these things

CONTENTS

Why on earth did I join the Civil Service?	1
Life on (the other side of) the dole: 1 - Nottingham	3
Life on (the other side of) the dole: 2 - Walsall	5
Away from the coalface	12
Life on (the other side of) the dole: 3 - Wolverhampton	15
Swaziland	19
Back to "The Smoke"	45
An unhappy experience	52
Incomes Policy and Equal Pay	54
A pleasant interlude	71
A less pleasant experience	74
Brussels 1	81
The Iron Curtain and the Berlin Wall	95
King of the Castle: July to December 1981	99
Norman Tebbit stories	103
Life outside the office	108
Back to "The Smoke" 2	115
Something different: The Technical and Vocational Education Initiative (TVEI)	121
Eastern Europe	127
Brussels 2	136
A Royal Invitation	144
Staying in Brussels?	145
Japanese interludes	149
Back to the Real World	154
Important People	164
What did I achieve in nearly 40 years?	166
Appendix: Joint Statement on Co-operation between United Kingdom and Czechoslovakia in the Labour Market Area	170
Annex: Brexit: a Tragedy?	173
Acknowledgements	186

Why on earth did I join the Civil Service?

In my last year at University, like all my contemporaries, I had to decide what I wanted to do after I had graduated. We were in the early sixties. There was full employment, so there was no question of not finding work. My criteria were:

- I wanted to use my French;
- I wanted to work abroad;
- I would prefer not to spend most of my time in an office.

I soon realised that there was something missing there: work as a Parisian dustman would meet all the criteria!

I went along to the University Appointments Board. The man in charge suggested the Home Civil Service. My response was a resounding "No". What about the Foreign Office? That appealed, but, as a village blacksmith's son, I didn't think I came from the right background. "You won't get in if you don't apply" came the reply.

So I sent off for the forms. In the same pack, one could apply for the Administrative Class of the Foreign Office, the Home Civil Service and the Northern Ireland Civil Service, as well as an intermediate level called the Special Departmental Class, which was a graduate entry level for the Post Office, the Inland Revenue and the Ministry of Labour. I went through the procedures for all of these, which included a degree level examination (seven papers) which I took immediately after my final degree examination. I also applied for the Executive Class (A-level entry). I went for an interview for the Special Departmental Class. On my original application form I had put my choice as

1. Post Office;
2. Inland Revenue; and
3. Ministry of Labour.

On the long train journey down from Manchester to London for the interview, I looked at my choice again and decided that I would prefer the Ministry of Labour to the Inland Revenue and told them so at the interview.

The allocation of places was made on a competitive and strictly statistical basis, in accordance with the marks obtained in the examinations and interviews. When the results came I didn't have enough marks for the Administrative Class or the Post Office, but I did have enough marks for both the Inland Revenue and the Ministry of Labour. So, if I had not changed my mind on the train, I would have become a Tax Inspector!

I received the results while I was working in a *colonie de vacances* at Belley in France. In the meantime my options for employment had been narrowed down to

- An international salesman for Bata shoes;
- A Management Trainee at an insurance company in Manchester;
- Executive Officer in the Ministry of Power; and
- A Cadet in the Ministry of Labour.

I had already turned down a place at Manchester for a Teaching Diploma. I decided to join the Ministry of Labour and was 'posted' to Nottingham Employment Exchange as a trainee.

Life on (the other side of) the dole: 1 - Nottingham

I started work at the Midlands Region Staff Training Centre in Birmingham on 22 October, 1962. I feared that my career in the Civil Service might be short. The Cuban Missile Crisis was in full swing and there was a real risk that the Americans and Russians would start throwing nuclear bombs at each other with catastrophic consequences for everyone. Fortunately, there were some cool heads in the White House, who found a way out of the crisis.

Three days later, I went to Nottingham, for a five month training programme, where I did all the clerical and sub-clerical work that I was going to have to supervise later on. For the first six weeks, I worked on the Men's Employment Section – finding unemployed people jobs. As part of my training I went on a number of training courses in Birmingham. On the first of these, I met Geoff Davies, with whom I'm still in contact. (I next met him in a dance hall in Walsall and he invited me to join the Civil Service Sports Club in Wolverhampton, where I used to play table tennis and badminton. In 1968, I went to Wolverhampton as a Deputy Manager and Geoff became Finance Officer.)

Before I started work I had had four or five weeks kicking my heels, while the formalities were sorted out. However, towards the end of November, the Finance Officer came to me and said that I had three days leave, which I had to take before the end of the month. I said I didn't want them. Five minutes later, his boss, Wilf Tyas, came down to see me and said: "You've bloody well got to take them – the unions have fought hard for this and we don't want people not taking them".

There was a good atmosphere in the Nottingham office. Having been a student and often staying at the University late into the evening, I was quite shocked to find that by twenty past five in the evening the office was deserted and everyone had gone home. The exception was Fridays, when Unemployment Benefit was paid until six o'clock (for those who had recently found work). After that a number of us (all male, I think) retired to *The Royal Children*, a very old and substantial pub, about 300 yards from the office. Most stayed there until closing time, but I had to leave before a quarter to ten to catch the last bus to my home village of Wymeswold, twelve miles away. I often had difficulty keeping awake on the bus and, on one occasion, I woke up in Loughborough five miles past my destination.

In 1962 unemployment had already become quite high for the post-war period, but still well below 2% in Nottingham. In December, I transferred over to the Unemployment Benefit section to learn the mysteries of computation and payment of that benefit. On Boxing Day 1962 a big freeze started, which was to last until March or April the following year. In contrast to other parts of the country, there was very little snow in the Nottingham area, but all the construction workers were laid off and entitled to unemployment benefit.

Previously, unemployed people had been required to sign on Wednesdays and to come in on Fridays to be paid their benefit in cash – normally about £4 a week. The system could not cope with the increased numbers and so additional signing and pay days were introduced on Tuesdays and Thursdays. There was a convention that the same person could not act as pay clerk more than once a week. Consequently, they were scratching around for additional pay clerks and one week they had the bright idea of asking me to do it. I was very slow and had a queue stretching right out into the street. I also had an overpayment of £1 10 shillings, which did not go down very well. They never asked me to do it again!

Life on (the other side of) the dole: 2 - Walsall

In February 1963, I was told (there was no discussion or negotiation) that I was being "posted" like a letter to Walsall Employment Exchange. Having found it on the map, I made my way by train to Walsall on the first of March. There was thick snow on the ground. "Digs" had been arranged for me with Helen Cooper, who was a nice lady, but a terrible cook.[1]

At Walsall, my job title was "Employment Section Supervisor". It was a very good job. I was in charge of six staff. Our job was to try to "place" the 2000 people who were unemployed into jobs. I was 23 years old, but looked about 16. Two of my staff were over twice my age and approaching retirement, one was in his thirties and the others were under 21. The size of the section was perfect for a first supervisory job: I was a "manager" – there was little personal performance – but it was manageable. Under the guidance of the Deputy Manager, Don Young, who had been a former staff inspector, I was very strict – much stricter than I would dare to be in later life!

I did not like Walsall all that much, as a place to live, but from a professional point of view, it was ideal. I learned quickly that the people of Walsall did not consider that they lived in the Black Country. Indeed it was remarkably self-contained. It had a population of about 100000. There were only two firms who employed more than 1000 people – Talbots, who made steel tubes and Crabtrees, who made electrical goods. There were

---

[1] It was common practice in those days for single men working away from home to take lodgings – bed, breakfast and evening meal, plus full board at weekends – in private houses. Helen Cooper lived with her husband Ron and three children in a pleasant three- or four-bedroomed terraced house about 10 minutes' walk from the centre of Walsall. She had one other tenant. During my first two years at Manchester University I had lived in similar accommodation. There three of us shared one bedroom, two Laotian students shared a second bedroom, while an older Indonesian student had a single bedroom. In addition, three other students had a flat in the attic!

several firms employing between 200 and 500 people, mainly in foundries or engineering industries. Walsall had traditionally been a leather town and there were still a few tanneries and many small firms producing leather goods. (They were always short of workers – the jobs were skilled and not very well paid!) Apart from Avery's factory, making weighing scales, just over the border in West Bromwich, nearly everyone worked in Walsall. Geographical mobility was almost non-existent, to the extent that people in the suburb of Bloxwich did not want to work in the main part of Walsall and vice versa. However, this simplified our task, which was to find workers for the employers in Walsall and to find work for the workers in Walsall.

By the time I went to Walsall, the unemployment situation had deteriorated. We were into the third month of construction lay-offs and the underlying economic conditions were unfavourable. There was talk of half a million unemployed nationally.[2] In those circumstances, it was very difficult to place anyone in employment. Part of my job was to get to know the employers in the town. I had not been there too long, when I went to see the Managing Director of Frosts, a medium-sized company that made electric fires. The winter was over, but the national economic situation was gloomy. He asked me if I had seen the figures for the construction industry (which, of course, I hadn't). He said that they were beginning to improve and that the rest of the economy would follow. He was right: three years later, Roy Jenkins, as Chancellor of the Exchequer, had to take measures to damp down the economy.

Throughout most of 1963, the employment situation remained difficult, particularly for unskilled workers, who

---

[2] I have been unable to check this assertion: I have only been able to find detailed records going back to 1971!

formed the majority of our clients. Towards the end of that year, we received an "order" (a request for workers) from McAlpines for 400 workers to work on the new motorway junction (between the M5 and the M6) that was being built just south of Walsall. This was an unbelievable bonus. From then on the employment situation improved rapidly. As a consequence, until the staff inspectors caught up with us, there was a surplus of staff on the Unemployment Benefit Section. One day, early in 1964, Don Young asked me what I would do, if I had an extra member of staff. I said that the staff I had could cope with the normal work, but an extra person could do development work contacting employers for vacancies, give more publicity to our services and interview all the long-term unemployed. A bright and dynamic young woman called Jenny came to work for me and did all those things. Word soon got round about the interviews and, miraculously, many people found jobs and ceased to claim Unemployment Benefit.

By the summer of 1964, the employment situation had completely turned round and employers were desperately short of labour. The owner of the printing firm next door to the Employment Exchange told my manager, Mr Arnold, one day in my presence, that this country would never be any good until there were ten men for every nine jobs! The situation in the printing industry was very difficult at that time: the trade unions operated a strict "closed shop", which stifled most changes in working practices.

It was about that time that the Personnel Manager from Avery's telephoned me to say he was so desperate for labour that he would take on anyone who could walk to the counter. It so happened that the previous week, George Burdett, the supervisor of the Unemployment Benefit Section, had brought the "claims unit" (or file) of an unemployed man to me. This man had been unemployed continuously since the mid-fifties. He asked me if there was anything I could do. With that in mind, I arranged for this man to be sent to Avery's. The Personnel Manager never spoke to me again. Sometime later my deputy, Lilian Jones, confided in me, with some satisfaction, that the man from Avery's had told her that he preferred to speak to her, because she understood better what he required.

After two years doing that job, I was told it was time for a change "in the interests of my career". (How often did I hear that over the next thirty years?") There had been a staff inspection and it had been decreed that the Unemployment Benefit and Finance Sections would be combined into one post. (The number of unemployed people claiming benefit had fallen from over two thousand to about 250.) I was to occupy this new post. Whereas my previous job was self-contained and easily manageable, this new job was messy. I had two offices, one above the other. The staircase was about thirty yards along corridors from each. The peak time for each was Friday, when Unemployment Benefit was paid. While the inspectors were right, that it did not warrant two full-time people, it was a big job for one.

The staff numbers had been cut right down, so I had to "muck in" with some of the clerical work. I didn't mind that, because I had learned to do that at Nottingham. There were some difficult computations which had to be certified by a supervisor (i.e. me) but, as I never understood them, I had to take the word of the clerical officer who did. The reduction in staff numbers also meant that, on one occasion – and for the second time in my career – I had to act as pay clerk. I made at least one overpayment and I decided that I was going to get the money back. So, foolishly, one dark Friday evening, I walked round the back streets of one of the poorer parts of

Walsall and knocked on a door. An 'old' woman, who I assumed was the claimant's mother, invited me into the living room. There was a coal fire with a metal fire-guard. On the fire-guard were half a dozen unwashed babies' nappies, hanging out to dry. I didn't get the money, but I can still remember the stench!

The finance part of the work was interesting, at least with hindsight! Everything was paid in cash. Every night before going home, I had to count the money left in the safe physically. If there was sixpence missing, it had to be found; likewise, if there was sixpence too much, it had to be explained. If, after several hours of searching, it could not be found, an error sheet had to be made. Such sheets were a mark of incompetence and severely frowned upon. The safe had to be locked at all times, when I was not in the room. Don Young, the Deputy Manager, made regular checks of that and random checks of the balance in the safe.

It was my job to estimate the imprest, which was the amount of money we needed to get from the bank each week. During the year I was there, it did not vary very much – between £700 and £800. Again, it was severely frowned upon, if on Friday evening, there was too much money left in the safe. Against that possibility had to be weighed the extreme embarrassment of running out of money. Fortunately, I never heard of that happening to anyone! Every Thursday I had to go to the bank with a colleague. The colleague was not there for my protection, but to make sure I did not run off with the money. We had a taxi and were supposed to vary our time and route. (The latter was difficult, as the bank was only about 500 yards away.) Once we had got the money, it was put in a leather bag. This was locked and chained to my wrist with another lock and key. My colleague had the keys. At that time, the protection of public money was more important than the protection of employees. (I'm pleased to say that policy was reversed some years later.)

I had not been doing these two jobs all that long, when the "Powers That Be" decided that they wanted to send a young woman, who had not successfully completed her probation, to do the Unemployment Benefit part of my job. I was left as Finance Officer, which was less than half a full-time job. Throughout my career, I was always able to see things that needed doing, so I was never left with nothing to do. On the whole I think in that way I was able to make a positive contribution to whatever I was doing. Critics might say that this was a means of avoiding things I did not want to do. For the only time, in my career this ability to find things to do was severely tested, but I still didn't get round to sorting out the pile of spare keys, which were in the old safe and which Don Young asked me to sort out.

It was during this period that I was asked to go to Darlaston, a few miles down the road, to work as Manager for two weeks: the Manager and his Deputy were both going to be away. (I think the Manager was sick and his Deputy on leave.) The Darlaston office was very small: there were two members of staff, apart from the two who were away. On the other hand, Darlaston was home to one of the largest heavy engineering firms in the Black Country – Rubery Owen. One of the responsibilities of the Manager was to keep on good terms with their Managing Director and I could expect a phone call from him at any time.

I felt quite important being a Manager, but was soon brought down to earth. Normally, in order to prevent fraud, three people needed to be involved in the computation and payment of Unemployment Benefit, but exceptionally this can be reduced to two. The most junior member of staff asked me politely, which part of the computation process – a routine clerical job – I wished to do. When I said I didn't mind, he explained that if I did one of them, I would have to be pay clerk as well. With my Nottingham experience in mind, I said I would do the other one!

I was disappointed to receive a phone call at the end of the first week to say that they were short of staff at Walsall and I had to go back.

***

During my three years at Walsall, my personal circumstances changed considerably. I had been living there for less than a year, when, on two of my rare trips back to my parents' home, I met my future wife, Jennifer, who lived in Nottingham. The consequence was that, every Friday evening I caught the blue number 6 Walsall Corporation bus to Sutton Coldfield in order to connect with the Midland Red X99 bus to Nottingham, which, conveniently, passed near to Jennifer's house. The fifty mile journey took three or four hours! The following day, we took another two buses to go to my parents' house in Wymeswold – 12 miles in an hour and a half! On Sunday afternoon and evening I made the return journey to Walsall!

I proposed to Jennifer, before she had ever been to Walsall. That may have been a good move on my part, because, when she visited it the following week for the first time, she was not impressed. We married in February 1965 and rented a flat in an old house in Glebe Street, Walsall. It was only about 100 yards downhill from our front door to the office, so I could almost literally roll out of bed and into work.

Jim Mackley

Away from the coalface

After three years in Walsall, I was posted to the Midlands Regional Office in Birmingham. This was a big region, stretching from Ross-on-Wye in the south and west to Boston in the east and Chesterfield in the north. For planning purposes, there were two regions: East and West Midlands. I was allocated to the Statistics and Regional Planning unit. I was in charge of a section with seven or eight Clerical Officers. Our main responsibility was to collect and collate the unemployment and other manpower statistics for the two planning regions. My team was responsible for the East Midlands and for combining these with those collected by Gerald Bodley's West Midlands team to produce a Midlands Regional figure. This figure had to be telephoned through to Headquarters in Watford by 5:00 p.m. on a Monday evening. I quickly realised that 100% accuracy was not possible, but I expected 99%. I expected the Clerical Officers to be 90% accurate with their first figure. These were checked and I expected the check to eliminate 90% of the errors.

We were not given expensive equipment. Each Clerical Officer had a large mechanical adding machine. As the main use for such machines in the rest of the Ministry was in Finance Offices, some of these machines were made to add up pounds, shillings and pence. The system for producing the regional unemployment figure usually worked perfectly, without my involvement. However, one evening, after 5:00 p.m., Stan Bates, the man responsible for producing the final figure, was left on his own, trying to make the figures balance. I offered to help. I picked up an adding machine and typed in the figures which he read to me. The result was a regional unemployment total of, something like, 195 pounds 17 shillings and 9 pence!

In July 1966, the Chancellor of the Exchequer, Roy Jenkins, announced severe economic restrictions to damp down the economy, which was overheating and so creating inflationary pressures. These measures had an immediate impact on the car industry, which employed thousands of people in the Midlands at that time. (It also had an impact on my meagre salary, which was frozen at around £1100 per annum gross for two years.) Most factories went on short time, which meant that the workers could claim Unemployment Benefit for the days they weren't working. I had to produce a daily report for the Deputy Regional Controller, Sandy Cowie.

We had in the office a manual calculating machine, with a handle, which only one or two people knew how to work. For a short time, we were given an electric machine, which did the same things, but made a loud noise. After a few months, I was offered a new machine on a trial basis. This was an electronic calculator, called Anita. It cost £2500, which was just under two and a half times my annual salary and about two thirds of the price we paid for our first house at about the same time. It was a beautiful machine, but was nearly as big as an old-fashioned portable typewriter. It could do exactly the same things as I can do now on the calculator app on my mobile phone!

One of the "Grade 4s" (Higher Executive Officers) was promoted and I had a long spell doing his job. I was expected to get promoted at the next promotion panel, but didn't. I had to revert to my old job and Dora Hyrnkievitch was brought in from managing one of the Black Country offices to be my boss. She was a jolly lady and we got on well together.

Every month, there was a Senior Officers' Meeting, chaired by Sandy Cowie. The participants were all the Grades 1, 2 and 3 in the region (Senior Principal, Chief Executive Officer and Senior Executive Officers – the latter included senior Employment Exchange Managers, covering the whole of the Midlands). The main purpose of the meetings was for the

Regional Office staff to provide information which could then be disseminated to all the Employment Exchanges in the region. While I was on temporary promotion, I was secretary for this meeting and I was required to produce the minutes of the meeting, within a very short time frame. The first time I did this, I met the deadline and took a day's leave the next day. I got a message from Sandy Cowie to go and see him as soon as I got back. When I did so, he told me in no uncertain terms that there were a number of inaccuracies and that I should check the minutes with all the Regional Office speakers before sending them out. That lesson stood me in good stead in future years.

Life on (the other side of) the dole: 3 - Wolverhampton

At the second attempt, I was promoted in the spring of 1968, the spring of (failed) revolutions, in particular in France and Czechoslovakia. Before the results of the promotion panel were announced, Sandy Cowie called me to his office and enquired where I would like to go, if I was promoted. (This was the first time I had ever been consulted on a "posting"!) I said that I didn't mind, providing that I wasn't sent to somewhere like Wolverhampton. Asked why I said that, I replied that we had just bought a house in South Birmingham. Wolverhampton was considered to be within daily travelling distance and consequently didn't qualify for removal expenses. Outcome: I was "posted" to Wolverhampton Employment Exchange as a Deputy Manager responsible for three Unemployment Benefit sections in three different locations, Finance, Redundancy Payments, repayments of Selective Employment Tax and Passports. The journey to Wolverhampton involved a train from King's Norton to Birmingham New Street and a second train from Birmingham to Wolverhampton. (The train that I often took ended up in Perth, but fortunately I always remembered to get off at Wolverhampton!)

The job was similar in scope to the last one I had at Walsall, but one rung further up the management scale. Since Roy Jenkins' July measures, unemployment had increased considerably: at £7000, the weekly imprest was ten times greater than at Walsall. All the other procedures were the same, except that it was now me who did the checks and someone else (the Finance Officer, Dave Bryan and later Geoff Davies) who was chained to the money bag during the journey back from the bank.

The Selective Employment Tax had been introduced by the Labour Government to favour employment in manufacturing industry. All employers paid the tax in respect of each employee. Employers in some industries, like transport, had their tax refunded, while those in manufacturing had their tax refunded with a premium. Large sums of money were involved, which it was the responsibility of the Executive Officers in charge to calculate. The classification of employers by industry gave rise to a large number of problems and disputes. A Standard Industrial Classification (SIC) had existed for many years and had been used for statistical purposes, in particular for the annual count of employees in employment. It was a good tool for that purpose, but was nowhere near precise enough to withstand legal challenges over large sums of money.

Manners were very formal in those days. I was "management" and the junior staff all called me "sir", including women who were thirty years older than me. (Thirty years later, secretaries thirty or more years my junior called me "Jim", if I was lucky!)

It was in Wolverhampton that I had my first, and possibly most serious brush with the National Press. The first Deputy Manager was on leave and the Manager, Reg. Pike, had asked me if I minded if he took the afternoon off to play golf, leaving me in charge. Wolverhampton had two MPs. Enoch Powell was the right wing Conservative MP for Wolverhampton South West and Renée Short was the left wing Labour MP for Wolverhampton North East. Enoch Powell had been a Minister in the previous Conservative Government, but was now best known for his views on (or against) immigration. On the day in question, it was Renée Short, who had made some comments on the radio about the employability of young black people. Staff in local offices were not supposed to speak to the Press. I went to visit one of my Unemployment Benefit Sections which was outhoused in a different part of Wolverhampton. When I got back to the main office, a scruffy reporter from *The Sun* was firmly ensconced in the office of the third Deputy Manager, who was even less savvy than I was in that situation. He had been talking to the reporter and had said some things that I thought he ought not to have said. I did my best to retrieve the situation and, in fact, the report that appeared the next day was not too bad.

It was normal throughout my Civil Service career, for constituents to write to their MP to complain about perceived mistakes or faults or failures in the system. The MP would then normally write to the Minister and ask for an explanation. An investigation would then follow. Enoch Powell received a letter from a constituent about failures at our Wolverhampton office. (I don't think the word "alleged" is necessary in this case.) Instead of following the normal cumbersome procedure, the MP sent the letter on to Reg. Pike, with a short polite note, saying that he was sure there must have been a mistake and asking him to look into it. I did not like Enoch Powell's political views, but I respected the way he handled this matter.

The first Deputy Manager was transferred out of the office, after I had been there for a few months, and I was made deputy until they found someone more experienced to replace him. My only direct responsibilities in this new job were for the secretaries, the switchboard and premises matters, but I also had responsibility for allocating staff to the various sections and the other two offices at Cannock and Bilston in the Wolverhampton area. I did not find it as satisfying as my line management job.

Unlike my first office at Wolverhampton, this office had an outside window with a view. In the foreground was the coal yard for the two railway stations. Then there was the railway line and Wolverhampton Low Level station, followed by another railway line and Wolverhampton High Level Station. In the background were a number of power station cooling towers. This was not a pretty sight and a marked contrast with the view from my next office in Swaziland!

Swaziland

I had only been at Wolverhampton three months, when a vacancy was advertised for a "Manpower Planning Specialist" in Swaziland. The requirements were quite vague. In the early part of my career, I applied for all jobs abroad that I was possibly qualified for. Indeed I was put on a shortlist in around 1965 for a transfer to the newly created Foreign and Commonwealth Office. (I received a letter about seven years later to say that I was still on the list, but nothing since.) Having found out where Swaziland was on the map I applied for the job. I received an acknowledgement, but then heard nothing for several months.

Suddenly, there was a flurry of activity in January and I was required to go for interview in London in a few days' time. Among the people on the panel was a woman from the Ministry of Overseas Development (ODM) and Dr Richard Jolly, from the Institute of Development Studies at the University of Sussex. By this time I knew that I would be required to make a survey of the supply and demand for manpower in Swaziland. In answer to a question about how I would go about this, I said that I would visit all the employers in the country. My heart was in my mouth in case they asked me how I was going to do that, when I couldn't drive. Very soon after that, at the age of 29, I had my first driving lesson!

Not long after that, Richard Jolly sent me a long letter, saying that *he* would not be making the final decision on the appointment, but recommending a long list of publications that I should read, if I got the job. (Dr Jolly had done a similar survey in Zambia.) At the time I wasn't sure whether the letter meant that I *would* get the job or whether it was meant to tell me not to think of applying for such a job, without knowing more about it. Sometime later, I received a letter saying my name had been forwarded to the Swaziland Government, but the appointment was in their hands.

Again, there was a long break, when nothing happened. Indeed, I had put Swaziland out of my mind and started making plans for the summer. Then, around Easter, some three months after my interview in London, I was called to an urgent meeting with the woman from ODM to make arrangements for going to Swaziland. While I was in London, I met Godwin Nxumalo,[3] who was the Swazi official, responsible for running the two employment exchanges. He was the first Swazi I met: he had a round brown face and smiling eyes. He was typical of many Swazis, though there were many others who were not so attractive, of which more later. I also met a peer of the realm for the first time. I don't remember his name, but he was much involved with Overseas Development. I remember being worried about how to address him.

At the meeting with ODM, the woman asked when I could start. I said I would prefer to go in June, after Jennifer, my wife, had taken the 'A' Level examination she had been studying for. The reply came that, at the previous interview, I had implied that I would be available in about six weeks. I did not give in then, but in subsequent correspondence I relented to say that I would go within six weeks of getting a contract with the Swaziland Government. ODM kept up the pressure and pinned me down to a date. I finally agreed that we would arrive in Swaziland on Friday 30th May 1969. I still did not have a contract with the Swaziland Government. In the meantime, we had let our house in Birmingham on a 17 month tenancy!

---

[3] 'Nx' is pronounced by making a clicking sound at the front of the mouth.

By this time we had tried to learn a bit about Swaziland, but the books we read gave contradictory impressions. The semi-official publications stressed the quality of public and private services: water, electricity, telephone, schools, banks and shops etc. Others pointed out how wild (or 'natural') the country was. One quote I remember almost put me off going: *Snakes abound in Swaziland.* (In fact I saw only two or three all the time we were there; Jennifer saw rather more, the last of which she beheaded with a spade.)

We had been in an aeroplane only a few times before we went to Swaziland. We flew from Elmdon aerodrome near Birmingham. At that time the future Birmingham International Airport consisted of a runway and a shed for passenger arrivals and departures. We had a very short flight to Heathrow, a few hours' wait and then a 17-hour overnight flight with South African Airlines (SAA) to Johannesburg. It was unusual for the British Government, who were paying, to use SAA, rather than the national (and nationalised) carrier, British Overseas Aircraft Corporation (BOAC). Because of their apartheid regime, SAA were banned from flying over many African countries, so we had a refuelling stop in the Cap Verde Islands, which were Portuguese.

Peter, our elder and, at that time, only son, was a month over two years old. Like us he had been subjected to a number of injections. These must have been traumatic, because 17 months later, on the return journey, he was running round Johannesburg Airport, shouting "no more 'jections!" On the journey out, we think it was his ears that were the problem. Whatever it was, he cried noisily most of the way to the Cap Verde Islands. He had only just gone to sleep when we had to wake him up to get off the plane.

I shall never forget my first experience of Africa. We got off the plane. It must have been around midnight. It was dark and very, pleasantly, warm. Palm trees surrounded the brightly lit area where black men with smiling faces served us with drinks. Certainly one of the most exotic experiences of my life! How boring it is to be a civil servant!

We arrived in Johannesburg and had two nights in a hotel there before we were due to catch the 8:00 a.m. Swazi Air flight to Matsapa, near Manzini in Swaziland. So far, everything had gone like clockwork. When we arrived at Johannesburg airport – we were among the first potential passengers for that flight – we were told that, as we had not confirmed our onward flight, we were not on the flight list. (No-one had told me that this had to be done – presumably, it was assumed that 'everyone knew!') We were told to wait on standby, in case the flight was not full. Things were looking good until a few minutes before the deadline, when a Scotsman, his wife and three children turned up, taking the five seats which I had thought were still available. I had either miscalculated or been misinformed, because in the end we were allowed on the plane.

The small plane, a DC3, flew just over the tops of the forests. The following may not be right – it doesn't seem possible – but my recollection is that when I went to the toilet, I could see the trees through the toilet hole. We were taken to the *Swazi Inn*, a mile or two outside Mbabane, the capital. We were to stay in the *Swazi Inn,* until the Swaziland Government found us accommodation.

We were put in a rondavel, twenty yards or so from the main building. I arranged a telephone call to my mother in England to tell her we had arrived. The phone rang about ten minutes later and it was so clear that my mother sounded as though she was in the next room. (I subsequently found out that this was in stark contrast to telephone calls to the south of Swaziland. For these it was necessary to call the operator, who had a wind-up machine to dial the number. It could take several hours to get a call through and, even then, the reception was not good.)

We were then introduced to South African restaurant menus. These typically, for a fixed price, consisted of nine or ten items from which one could choose freely. The idea was that one would choose three courses, but there was nothing to prevent one from eating one's way all through the menu, as my counterpart, Tennyson Nkonyane, did on one occasion.

I was allocated to the Economic Planning Unit in the Swaziland Government. The Head of the unit was Dr Jule, a Norwegian, whom, with little originality, we called *Father Christmas*. The Senior Economist was Ralph Clarke, a rather outspoken man, who had spent most of his career on international development work mostly in Africa. The other members of the team were James Nxumalo, who had a master's degree at an American University, but very little influence, and Michael Zwane, who was a very quiet graduate, whom I was supposed to train to take over from me when I left. There were also two secretaries, one of South African origin and one Swazi.

On the Sunday after we arrived – around the 1st June, so almost the middle of winter – we were invited to go for a picnic with Dr Jule, Ralph Clarke and his wife, Jenny, and a young British graduate, Bruce Dinwiddy, who was due to return back to England at the end of his secondment from the Overseas Development Institute (ODI) a non-governmental organisation.[4] We had a picnic out in the country, not far from Mbabane. Dr Jule produced a bottle of South African bubbly. Bruce commented that he was looking forward to getting back to Europe, where he could drink 'real champagne'. (I, on the other

---

[4] Bruce Dinwiddy went on to have a distinguished career in the Foreign and Commonwealth Office, including High Commissioner in Dar es Salaam (1998 – 2001) and Governor of the Cayman Islands (2002 – 2005).

hand, had never tasted champagne outside France – a bottle of cheap red wine was a luxury in those days.)

My first working day was the Queen's birthday. We were invited for drinks on the High Commissioner's lawn. A young woman asked me what I wanted to drink. Not knowing what to say, I asked for a Martini. I was brought a drink which was not the Martini Rosso that I was expecting, but which I liked very much. So began my brief love affair with gin and tonic. I subsequently discovered that the young woman who took my order was Sue Webster, who, along with her husband, Stan, has now been our friend for over 50 years.

Our first seven weeks in Swaziland was dominated by domestic matters. I bought a car – a Renault Caravelle – which most people thought was the name of an aeroplane. It was a beautiful red car, but not very reliable. I managed to pass my test, but probably did not deserve to - I'm fairly sure I would have been failed, if I had been black.

The Caravelle on the road to Pigg's Peak

The main preoccupation, however, was housing. The British Government paid my salary and allowances, but the Swaziland Government was contracted to provide us with suitable accommodation. It had been the tradition in colonial days for expatriate staff to be housed in good quality Government accommodation. We went there a year after independence and the new Swazi Government had decided to allocate these houses to local staff, when the expatriates left. Consequently, there was a shortage of accommodation.

In the meantime Jennifer was stranded with Peter in a hotel, which was very nice, but too far from Mbabane to contemplate walking there – it was on the side of a mountain and there were no pavements, but there were fast cars and bad drivers. We had been there a couple of weeks, when Ralph Clarke advised me to write to the Permanent Secretary for Establishments and Training, Christopher Dlamini, to remind him that they were supposed to provide me with accommodation. At about the same time, we were invited to go to look at an apartment. Access to the building was via a footbridge, which had a ten-foot drop either side of it. We turned that down, because we thought it was unsuitable for a two-year old boy. We were fortunate that for two separate weeks we were lent beautiful houses by people that we had not met before, but who had heard of our plight and were going away.

After we had been there six weeks, things came to a crunch. We decided to go to the British High Commission to complain. We saw Ray Stevens, who was the Executive Officer. We told him our story and asked "What is the British Government going to do about it?" "Not much," said Jennifer afterwards, but she was wrong. The next afternoon I was summoned to Mr Dlamini's office. He was a big fierce-looking man, with a fearsome reputation. He was accompanied by Mr Smit, the South African Principal responsible for staffing matters. The High Commissioner had written to Mr Dlamini, pointing out their responsibility for accommodation and threatening to withdraw me (meaning 'send us home!'), if they did not find accommodation within a week. Mr Dlamini was furious (or at least pretended to be). He said that if I had a problem I should come to him, rather than go running to the British Government. Fortunately, I was able to say that I had written to him, but had not received a reply. Mr Smit, to his credit, confirmed my story. The rest of the interview consisted of quite aggressive questioning, whereby Mr Dlamini appeared to be weighing up whether or not I was expendable. The interview ended with him saying that, as I knew, he had no property available, but, if I could find anything reasonable within the next week, he would rent it for us. A few days later, one of my acquaintances found out about a small house that was vacant. It belonged to a Jewish businessman and property owner, Mr Goldblatt. He lived in the big house next door. This house had originally been built for his Portuguese servant. It was not nearly as grand as the houses that most of my colleagues lived in, but we were lucky to find it and it was certainly preferable to the alternative, which was to be sent home!

We moved in there the following week. At the bottom of the garden was a tin shed, where a girl of about nineteen, Sarah, lived with her little boy, who was a bit younger than Peter. (The boy's father also lived there, but nobody was supposed to know that!) Sarah asked if she could stay on as our servant. Although the conditions were appalling, the alternatives, as far as she was concerned, were worse.

We had a reasonable sized garden, though small by the standards of my colleagues. I was 29 and used to doing my own gardening. Every Saturday boys would come knocking at our door, asking if they could do our gardens. One day, a boy called John came round. He was slightly disabled, but had "a bit more about him" than most of the boys. He said he needed the work to pay for his schooling. I took him on and he did a good job. One day, I decided that I wanted part of the garden grassing over. The grass there was mainly Kikuyu grass, which spread horizontally. "Very good, sah", he said. He promptly went out of the gate and dug up some of the grass verge. Within a very short time, I had my lawn, because the grass he planted spread very quickly.

A feature of the garden, which puzzled us when we first moved in, was a dry concrete channel that ran diagonally across the garden. We soon found out what it was for, when the first rains came in September. (It "knows how" to rain in Swaziland – the average annual rainfall in Mbabane is 1337 mm, which falls usually in the summer months between September and April.) Our house was situated below street level, so, when it rained, the water used to gush through the garden gate. Some of it then went into the channel and rushed through the garden and out into the end of Mr Goldblatt's garden, which was further downhill. Some of the rest went into the drain at the corner of the house, but most brought with it a large quantity of red sandy soil and deposited it on the concrete driveway at the side of the house.

A feature of our garden that was admired by all our friends was a tree. It was a tall tree – I don't know what sort – but it was entwined by three different creepers with burgundy, orange and yellow flowers and was spectacular for long periods of the year.

There was also a black cat living on our premises. We fed it. Periodically it mated with the Siamese cat belonging to Mr Goldblatt. The mother was too proud to keep her mongrel offspring, so she deposited them with the father in our carport. We did not have many problems with exotic wildlife, but we did have a perennial problem with beetles in the kitchen. On one occasion **one** locust got into our bedroom. In the space of a few hours, it devoured Jennifer's large wicker sewing basket. On another occasion a chameleon – grey to match the sky – crawled ever so slowly across our washing line.

Chameleon

Our offices were in Allister Miller Street. From my office window I had a view over the town to the Prime Minister and High Commissioner's residences in the hills on the outskirts of the town. My basic UK annual salary at that time was about £1800. For the "hardship" of living in Swaziland, with its wonderful climate and beautiful scenery, I was paid another £800 or so, tax free, plus accommodation and other expatriate perks. When I contrasted that with the view from my window in Wolverhampton, I found it difficult to believe my good fortune.

Allister Miller Street, Mbabane, 1970

We shared the building with the Ministry of Foreign Affairs. One day Jennifer had been to see me, accompanied by Peter. She was standing waiting for the lift with a senior Swazi diplomat. Suddenly Peter asked: "Mummy, why has that man got a white face?" Fortunately, the man saw the funny side of it – or he was a good diplomat! Sometime later Peter went to the private Nursery School. Most of the children there were white. One day he came home and said he'd got a new friend. He spent some time describing this boy to his mother, but didn't think to say that the boy was black.

Workwise I was floundering at the beginning. I had only a vague idea of what I needed to do and even less of an idea of how I was going to do it. It was however clear that different parts of the Swaziland Government had different ideas as to what they wanted me to do. Dr Jule had no particular interest in what I was supposed to be doing. This became clear to me when, after I'd been there a few weeks, he came to me and asked, as they were very busy, would I help out and do some project appraisals. When I replied that I didn't know how to do it, he was surprised, because he thought I had a post-graduate qualification in Economics. This was strictly true – I had obtained a GCE A level in Economics at Bourneville College of Further Education in 1968, six years after I obtained my Bachelor's degree. Dr Jule implied that he only agreed to my appointment because he thought I was an economist and I might be a useful pair of hands.

Things changed after I had been there six or eight weeks. David Anderson from the Ford Foundation came on a visit to Mbabane. I was introduced to him and for some reason he seemed to take a liking to me – or felt sorry for me. He had a colleague, Bob Thomas, who had been doing manpower surveys all over Africa, most recently in Tanzania. David arranged for Bob to come to Mbabane a few weeks later. Bob was an economist, but an action man, rather than a purist. He had a method: it was rough and ready, but it was "guaranteed" to produce results in a few months rather than years. (I subsequently discovered that Richard Jolly had done a similar study in Zambia, using a computer, but two years' later the information was locked into the computer and was not accessible.)

I went to Manzini with Bob Thomas to meet the Swaziland Employers' Federation. They were on the defensive, as the objective of the manpower exercise was to prepare for the replacement of expatriate workers by Swazi workers in the private sector, in particular in skilled and management posts. They insisted that I should ask, in every case, what qualifications and how many years' training would be required for a Swazi person to do the job. This was very tiresome, but I did it on most occasions.

The winter in Swaziland was beautiful: cold nights and bright sunny days, with the temperatures changing from 0 to 20 degrees and back again in a few hours. The rainy season normally started in September and lasted about six months. In 1969 the rains began in September, but ended on Christmas Day – we had no significant rain in the remaining ten months that we were there. The rainy season coincided with the period, when I was doing the field work for my manpower survey. During this period I visited all the major employers in the country and obtained information about all their skilled and managerial jobs.

By this time, Michael Zwane had been replaced by Nkonyane. He had a first name, Tennyson, but most people referred to him just as 'Nkonyane'. He accompanied me on some of these trips. Although I am a linguist, I decided that there was no mileage in learning the local language, SiSwati. Nkonyane had other ideas. One evening in a hotel, he explained to me that SiSwati is a rhyming language. For example, there are two expressions for 'where': *Lipi li* and *Upi u*, which rhymed with the noun. Apart from the standard greeting (*Sawubona*) and the response (*Jebo*), that is about all I learned. However, that came in useful. Towards the end of our stay, we decided to go on a 'grand tour' of Swaziland. Somewhere in the south of the country we took a wrong turning: there was a myriad of unmarked, dirt roads in Swaziland. We arrived at an unmarked cross-road and didn't know which way to go. As often seemed to be the case, a Swazi came out of the bush. I asked him if he spoke English. He replied in a perfect Oxford accent: "No!" So I used my complete SiSwati vocabulary to ask: *Upi u Hlatikulu?* (Where is Hlatikulu?) He beamed at me and pointed in the right direction.)

Nkonyane was an interesting character. He did not have the formal education of Michael Zwane, but he was well connected politically and had a lot of drive and determination. (He actually said that I did too!) He had a drink problem and sometimes came round to our house in the evening, asking to see Jennifer. When she could, she hid in the bedroom and pretended to be sleeping.

In parallel with my survey, the Minister of State for Establishments and Training, Christopher Dlamini's boss, set up a Localisation Committee. I was a member. The aim of this committee was similar to that of my survey: to draw up a timetable for replacing foreign public servants by Swazi nationals. There were some interesting exchanges, in particular between the Minister and the (British) Director of the Public Works Department. On one occasion, the latter failed to attend a meeting, because he had broken a leg. When asked subsequently how he had done it, he replied: "I slipped, when kicking the cat!" Sympathy quickly evaporated!

I was also involved with the Ministry of Education. During my interview in London for the job, Richard Jolly had asked me a question about education policy. I had hazarded a reply and then said that I thought that would be a matter for the Ministry of Education to deal with. I have never forgotten Richard's reply: "Education is much too important to be left to Ministries of Education!" I had a good relationship with the Director of Education, Hennie Esterhuizen – I bought my golf clubs off him – but the Permanent Secretary often turned to me for an opinion rather than his officials. One of these was Telfer Blacklock, one of my golfing partners. He was, like me, a Higher Executive Officer (HEO) in the British Civil Service, but he was kept strictly in his place by his hierarchy.

In the spring of 1970 I was asked to write an article for the Swaziland Teachers Journal. My article (complete with a photo and adverts!) is reproduced below.

By this time, I had completed the fieldwork for my survey and now had the job of tabulating the results. I don't remember the detail now, but, along with Jennifer, we produced some tables, based on the International Standard Classification of Occupations (ISCO). The title of my report was to be: *Analysis of Swaziland's Manpower Resources and Requirements: 1969-1974*. I believe the *Analysis of Swaziland's Manpower Resources* was good, but the rest was based on heroic assumptions, in particular on economic growth. The economists in our unit refused to produce a forecast, so Bob Thomas said I should do it. I chose 5% per annum.

(B) TRAINING AND EMPLOYMENT

Educating for Employment
BY J. W. MACKLEY

THE QUESTION — "What are we educating for?" — is not a new one. Nor is it possible to give a universal answer to it. In some societies it is argued, quite reasonably, that secondary or even higher education is the right of every child, that every individual should be developed to his or her full potential and according to his individual talents, irrespective of the costs. In other, poorer, countries it is necessary to look more critically at what is involved before following such a course in order to ensure that investment in education brings the maximum possible benefit to the community as a whole.

The cost of education is high. In Swaziland, in 1969/70, education will have consumed about 17% of the annual recurrent budget, in addition to the contributions made by missions and other benefactors. Expansion of education is not just a question of putting up new buildings. It is a question of supporting the high (recurrent) costs, which have to be met year after year. Aid agencies are usually willing to assist generously with the initial (capital) expenditure where they consider that the community will benefit from new buildings or the expansion of existing facilities. They are not generally very willing, indeed it is not their function, to foot the bill when it comes to the bread and butter question of paying for the services provided, on a regular annual basis. Nor can it be argued, glibly, that "the government" will find the money. Certainly, having given its approval to a project, the government will make the payment, but the government's revenue is limited and, like the private household, it can only determine how the funds available are to be spent. Money spent on education is consequently not available for expenditure on other items such as better health services, better roads, better housing or the development of agriculture, all of which deserve a high priority in the allocation of the country's scarce resources. It is important, therefore, to ensure that, in denying people's other needs in favour of education, the country's educational effort should be directed towards rational and clearly defined targets, rather than towards targets which, though admirable, might not be the best in the current situation.

An analysis of the employment situation in Swaziland shows two contrasting elements, which though common to many other countries at the time of independence, make the problem of educating for employment all the more difficult to solve. On the one hand there are insufficient local people trained to man all the top posts in industry and commerce, while on the other hand less than one third of the population of working age is in wage employment. Unfortunately, with about 55% of the African population under 20 years of age¹ and a high birth-rate, there is no likelihood of employment opportunities in the so-called 'modern' sector growing at a faster rate than the number of young people coming into the employment field. Thus the majority of young people will spend their lives, not in factories, offices or on the

¹*Report on the 1966 Swaziland Population Census.*

J. Mackley (Manpower Planner).

large sugar estates and forests, which constitute the 'modern' sector, but in a more traditional environment. It is essential that their needs should not be forgotten. While not presuming to tell teachers how to achieve their ends I believe that they should feel well satisfied if at the end of primary school young people are equipped with the practical sense, and, above all, the right mentality to tackle one of the major tasks facing the country today: the development of the rural economy.

While it is important not to idealize the 'modern' sector and not to encourage young people to flock in from the rural areas to become unemployed in the towns, it is essential that development should not be further held back by a shortage of skilled and trained manpower. Until recently insufficient attention has been paid to the development of secondary education, so that there is much to be done before the country can have sufficient doctors, engineers, accountants, technicians, managers, specialist teachers, bricklayers and mechanics to meet its requirements. Indeed, until now, any programme involving the expansion of secondary and post-secondary education and training was almost certain to prove beneficial, because there was a shortage of all types of trained manpower. Even now, we have not fully ascertained how much more expansion of secondary education is needed or how many engineers or doctors it will be necessary to train to meet the country's manpower requirements. In order to rectify this situation and in order to ensure that, for example, the balance between arts and science graduates is right, a manpower survey is being carried out, at the time of writing. The survey, which covers all occupations in the professional, administrative, technical, clerical and skilled manual fields, will provide the basis of estimates of future demands for workers, occupation by occupation, over a five year period.

When people are trained it is important that their years of hard work should not end in frustration. If we have done our job properly, the output of secondary schools and post-secondary training establishments will relate to the demands of the employment market. But is not easy, even in a country the size of Swaziland, for everyone to be aware of the career and job opportunities that are available. Thus we must ensure that young people are given adequate guidance upon the careers that are open to them and direct assistance in finding employment. This means the introduction of an effective careers' guidance service and the development of the existing placement service.

To recap, I am proposing that investment in education should relate more closely than hitherto to the returns which the community can derive from it. This means ensuring that primary school-leavers are well prepared for life in the rural community, that secondary and post-secondary education and training are directly related to manpower requirements and that adequate provision is made for careers' guidance and for the placement of school leavers in employment.

———:::———

Jacaranda Shopping Centre

Stockists of:

GROCERIES AND PROVISIONS

ARMS AND AMMUNITION

RADIOS, RECORDS

RECORD PLAYERS

HARDWARE

LADIES
    LATEST FASHIONS

TRAVELWARE

COSMETICS

* * *

FARMERS IMPLEMENTS

and other

FARMERS REQUIREMENTS

VETERINARY SUPPLIES
AND EQUIPMENT

* * *

P.O. BOX 35   PHONE 14

STEGI.

MANZINI DRY CLEANERS

SWAZILAND'S EXPERT DRY CLEANING SERVICE

Fast and Efficient Service.
(Agent Cuthberts Shoe Repairs)

* * *

President Centre   Allister Miller St.
MANZINI   MBABANE.

DEPOTS THROUGHOUT
SWAZILAND

Dr Jule and Ralph Clarke had long since left. The unit had merged with the statistical office and become the Department of Economic Planning and Statistics. Our Permanent Secretary was James Nxumalo – the little fat boy in the corner, when I arrived. James reported directly to the Prime Minister, Prince Makhosini Dlamini. On one occasion in the early autumn, the Prime Minister sent for me. It being still very warm in the daytime, most expatriate officials wore "safari suits", sometimes with long trousers, sometimes with short trousers. The Prime Minister had a rule that no one was allowed to go to see him in short trousers. This was a problem for me, because on that particular day I was wearing shorts and Jennifer had the car. (The Prime Minister's residence and office were out of town, so I needed the car to get there.) I telephoned Jennifer and asked her to bring the car and a pair of trousers. The car was parked in our carport near the front door. In order to get the car on to the road, she needed to reverse round the corner of the house. At the corner of the house was a drain, which had lost its lid. In her haste, Jennifer got one wheel of the car stuck in this drain. Both she and Sarah, the maid, were pregnant, but, after a long delay, somehow they managed to get the car out of the drain.

When I had completed my report, I was asked to prepare a Cabinet Paper with policy proposals. This I did. I had to go to a Cabinet Meeting at the Prime Minister's Office to present the paper. It is remarkable, with my subsequent experience of the British and European Civil Service, that I went alone, unaccompanied by a more senior colleague. It is even more remarkable that I went into the meeting as soon as I arrived and was allowed to listen to the discussion on the previous item on the agenda. I don't remember the detail, but there was a proposal to do something in one part of the country, which might give rise to political difficulties. At that time the ruling party held all the seats in the Parliament. However, one of the

Ministers pointed out that the Opposition had nearly won that seat at the last election and argued against doing anything that would help their cause.

My Cabinet Paper was well received and my proposals in relation to education and training became Government policy. Glory days!

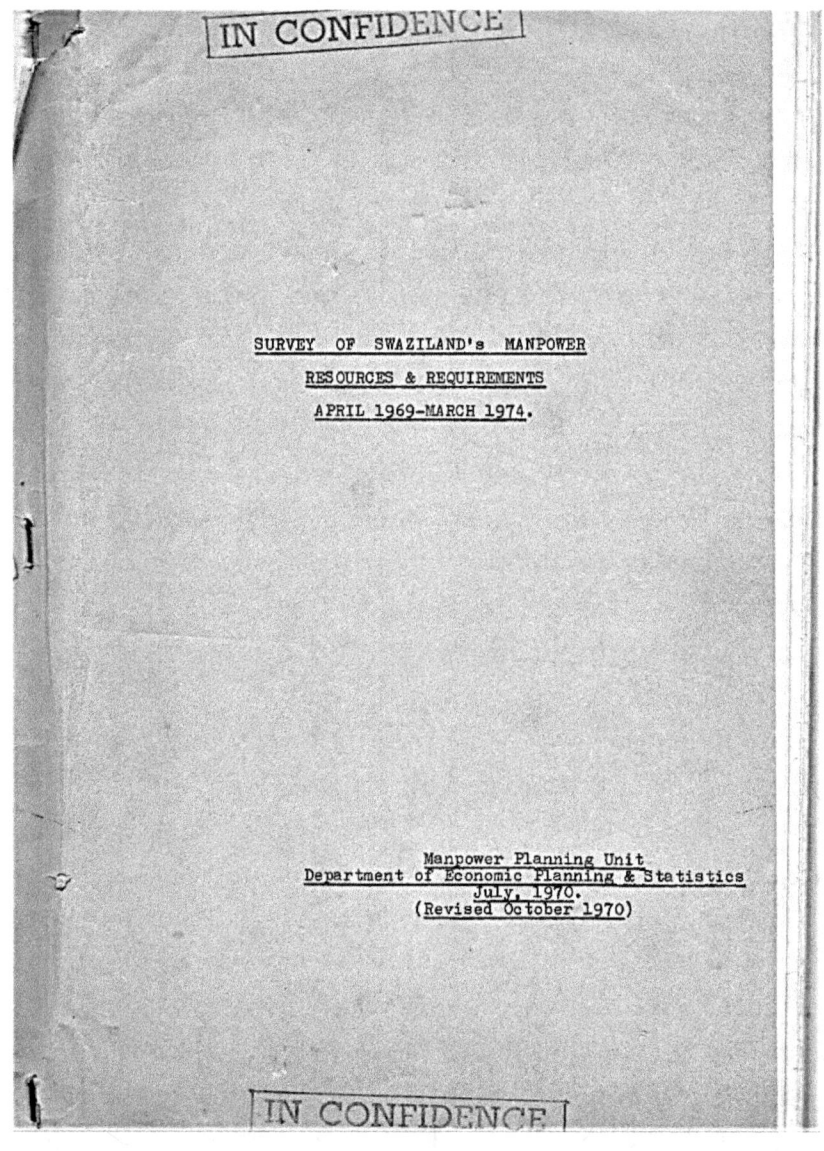

By this time my secondment was drawing to a close, so I was still on a high politically, when I left. My timing was good, because, early in 1971, there was a political crisis and the Government abandoned the planned approach I had outlined in favour of the traditional free for all.

Other stories

Swaziland had gained independence from the United Kingdom in September 1968. The following September, Princess Alexandra, the Queen's cousin, paid an official visit to Swaziland to mark the first anniversary of independence.

Swaziland's first independence anniversary September 1969 Princess Alexandra and King Sobhuza II are welcomed by Prime Minister Prince Makhosini Dlamini

There was a certain amount of rivalry between the different providers of development aid. Ralph Clarke was very outspoken. His departure was hastened by a comment he made, where he referred to the Chinese Nationalists (based in Formosa (Taiwan) under Chiang-Kai-Shek) as *the Blue Chinese*, as opposed to the *Red Chinese* of Mao Tse-Tung (as he was then known). This was considered to be somewhat derogatory and an embarrassment to Swaziland Government.

At the Queen's Birthday Party in June 1969, as I said above, I acquired a taste for gin and tonic. This lasted until September, when Bruce Dinwiddy invited us to his farewell party. (He didn't leave in the end, but he did have the party.) As usual I was drinking gin and tonic. Suddenly the room began to spin and I decided that I had to leave as soon as I could. At the same time the Secretary to the Cabinet came into the party, obviously (to everyone else) the worse for wear, having come from another party. I won't go into details of my state of health – suffice it to say that I have never wanted to drink gin again. The following weekend, the Secretary to the Cabinet organised a drinks do for David Anderson from the Ford Foundation, to which we were invited. When we arrived, the host took me on one side and said he was sorry I had taken offence at his behaviour at Bruce's party. He implied that when I "grew up" I would become more tolerant of other people's drinking habits. I don't think it had anything to do with his 'drink' problem, but he got his marching orders soon after and was replaced by a Swazi.

A car was essential in Swaziland. After a very short time, on the advice of Ralph Clarke, we bought our red Renault Caravelle. I had had several months of driving lessons in Birmingham, but had failed my driving test. Jennifer had also had a few driving lessons, but had not taken her test. As mentioned earlier, thanks to the indulgence of the driving examiner in Mbabane, I passed my test fairly quickly.

One Saturday, when we hadn't been there very long, we went for a drive along the tar road towards Johannesburg.

While we were out it started to snow – the only time we ever saw snow while we were there. On the way back – we were out of the snow – I suggested to Jennifer that she should drive the car for a while. I don't remember the detail, but we had an altercation, the result of which was that Jennifer refused to drive for several months.

Then another friend called Sue persuaded her to let her give her some driving lessons. They used to go to the football field. Jennifer practised reversing through the goal posts. One day she came back sheepishly to say that she had reversed past one goal post, but had scraped the side of the car on the other one! One Sunday, a few weeks later, I decided to practise a few holes of golf. It was a nine-hole course. Holes three to seven were out in the country. I decided to park the car alongside the bench by the third tee. I duly played my five holes and got back in the car. When I tried to drive off, I had forgotten about the bench and duly jammed the car against the bench. I went home and told Jennifer that I had scraped the car in the same place as she had. To which she replied that, if I had got out of the car to look, I must have scraped the other side – so the car had matching wings!

Jennifer took and passed her driving test a couple of weeks before Jonathan was born. The examiner took one look at her and said that it would be better to stick to the tar roads, which limited the scope considerably, in particular for uphill starts.

Earlier on in our stay, I used to park the car in the "main" car park near the bottom of our street, Gilfillan Street. One day I returned to the car park to go home for lunch. I got into the car and drove forward only to jam the car on the concrete area which had once contained an ornamental tree. I was completely stuck. However, as was so often the case in Swaziland, a large number of teenage boys appeared from nowhere and were much amused by my predicament. They took it upon themselves to rock the car until, somehow, miraculously, I was able to drive it off the plant pot.

The car park was nearly opposite the "drive-in" bakery. This was so named because it faced the bottom of the steep hill into the town centre on the main road from Johannesburg. On numerous occasions, drivers failed to stop at the end of the road and drove straight into the bakery in front of them. The standard of driving in Swaziland generally was very poor, with frequent reports of fatalities. That was one of the few reasons that I was not all that sorry to leave when we eventually had to do so.

When we had been there a few months, we decided that it would be "safe" to have another baby, in Mbabane and Jennifer became pregnant. We were entitled to use the private clinic on the outskirts of Mbabane. On the evening of 21 May 1970, Jennifer went into labour and I drove her to the clinic. Doctor Tredway, the doctor in charge of the clinic, also had a general practice in the centre of the town. The arrangement was that the staff in the clinic would telephone him when the baby was due to arrive.

I went to see Jennifer during my lunch break on 22 May and there was no sign of the baby. A friend, Lois Wardle, was looking after Peter, while Jennifer was in the clinic. I finished work at 4:45 pm and went to collect Peter. Lois had a group of friends with her and they insisted that I telephone the clinic to find out if there had been any developments. I said there was no point, as it had been only a few hours since I had seen her. They prevailed and I was told that Jonathan had arrived very quickly. All Dr Tredway did for his 250 rands (about £140) was to put on his white coat and catch him!

Before I got to the clinic, our friends, Stan and Sue, had gone to visit Jennifer. They asked, when she thought the baby would arrive. To their surprise, she replied that they could see him: he was in a cot at the side of the bed. Jennifer was very well treated in the clinic – most of the nurses were Cypriots. I fetched her out a few days later: it was the most glorious late autumn day, with a deep blue sky.

About three months later, Jonathan developed a lump on his neck. Dr Tredway said it needed an urgent operation, which he could do, otherwise there was a risk he would be paralysed. He performed the operation and every doctor who has seen the scar since has said that he did an excellent job. It was only afterwards that I heard the allegation that the night before, Dr Tredway had knocked down and killed the daughter of one of the Swazi Permanent Secretaries.

There was a good social life in Mbabane. Swaziland having achieved independence only a year before we arrived, the colonial clubs and social infrastructure were still in place, as were many of the members of the colonial administration. These were rapidly being replaced by a younger generation of more liberal expatriates, including me, who were there to support, rather than to govern.

After some hesitation because of its racist history, I joined the Mbabane club for the golf and tennis. The tennis was interesting. Because of the altitude (4000 feet above sea level) special tennis balls were used. I used to play two hours singles in the midday sun with my friend Colin, who was on secondment to the British High Commission.

There was a cinema club, run by the newer generation, which showed more "highbrow" or classical films. In particular Jennifer remembers with some dismay watching *Rosemary's Baby* when she was pregnant. There was also a Theatre Club, run by the older generation, which, as well as putting on theatre productions showed a monthly middle brow film. A few miles out of town was a Drive-in Cinema. This was a novel experience for us, which we have not repeated since. This showed films on the South African commercial circuit. Apartheid being in its hey-day, these films were heavily censored. One film that we watched was *Till Death us do part* featuring Alf Garnett, the racist Cockney bigot. (Tony Blair's father-in-law, Anthony Booth also starred as Garnett's socialist son-in-law.) We could never work out what the South Africans (or Swazis) made of this film.

We had several holidays in Mozambique, in and around Lourenço Marques (now Maputo). Mozambique at the time was a Portuguese province and LM was its capital. It was a beautiful European city and reminded me, at the time, of the South of France. Driving out of LM one was conscious of the rapid transition from a sophisticated capital to the African bush in the space of a few yards. One time we went on a boat trip to the island of Inhaca. We were about a mile from the shore, when the boatman switched off the engine and got out a pole and started punting us towards land. About a hundred yards from the shore, he announced that that was as far as he could take us and we would have to paddle the rest. This did not please Jennifer, who was pregnant and wearing tights. The island itself was the archetypal desert island: deserted apart from one bar, with pure white sand. One of my favourite memories!

The last time we went to Mozambique, some six months later, our son, Jonathan, was about 3 months old. We invited Sarah to go with us, partly as a treat for her – she had never seen the sea – and partly to look after Jonathan. We stayed in a hotel across the road from the beach. We had been there only a few days when Sarah began to complain of stomach pains. She said she had to go home. This we were reluctant to do. By the Thursday the pains had got worse and we had to take her to the hospital. We went to see her in hospital sometime later. I can still see the young male member of staff who said: "There was a baby!" It was only a few months since she had had her second child.

We also had a holiday in Natal in February 1970. While we were there we wanted to get some baby clothes for the baby Jennifer was expecting in May. We also wanted to get the car serviced in an authorised Renault garage. We had an enormous room in a good hotel, one road back from the sea front. There was a choice of eleven items on the menu and we could have eaten all of them, if we had wanted. I took the car to be serviced, but we never went shopping. The humidity was unbearable. The deal in the hotel was five nights for the price of four, but it was so humid that we left after four nights.

We drove south to a place called Hibberdene, where we stayed for a few nights including Jennifer's 26th birthday. The hotel was situated at the edge of a white sandy beach fringed with palm trees – idyllic. We spent one of the days further along the coast at Ramsgate or Margate! We spent the second week at a place called Chaka's Rock. The whole of that coast was perfect for a quiet beach holiday with Peter, who by now was nearly three years old. We had some political discussion with the English-speaking landlady. She was a great admirer of Enoch Powell, though he was a bit too much of a socialist for her liking.

Apart from the weekly *Times of Swaziland*, the only newspapers available were South African. I used to buy the *Sunday Times* because it had the English football results. I was struck by the strength of the antagonism expressed in that newspaper against the ruling Afrikaner Nationalist Party.

I used to write a letter to my parents every Monday. Amazingly, sometimes the two-way exchange took under a week, which meant that when I came to write, I had already received a reply to the previous week's letter. At that time, there was a Civil War in Nigeria/Biafra. My mother was worried that these events in Africa might cause us problems. I replied to ask if they were causing them any problems, as they were nearer than us!

Towards the end of my stay, Richard Jolly invited me to visit him in Zambia. We were due to go to see the Victoria Falls, but there was a family problem and so we stayed in Lusaka. Instead, Richard took me to an open air theatre, which was putting on a play about Che Guevara (whom I'd never heard of before!) The President, Kenneth Kaunda, was there and addressed the audience.

Back to "The Smoke"

A few months before I was due to leave Swaziland, Lawrie Levy in the Department of Employment Headquarters in London sent me a letter to say that "it was not in the interests of my career" to stay in Swaziland any longer. This implied that there was a career path laid out for me. What it really meant was that the "Powers That Be" in Personnel (or "Establishments", as it was still called) did not look favourably on people who went "swanning off" on overseas postings. I don't think staying on was an option, anyway, as James Nxumalo did not really want non-professionally qualified people in his Economic Planning Unit. I half-heartedly looked at some other similar jobs, including the British Virgin Islands, but did not apply for any.

We left in November 1970 and stopped off in Nairobi on our way back to England. Bob Thomas had told me that David Anderson, the Head of the Ford Foundation's African office, had a high opinion of me and wanted to see me. I had hoped that he might offer me a job. However, our plane from Manzini was delayed by a day and David had been called away by the time we got there, so I didn't see him.

Lawrie Levy told me that I would not be going back to the Midlands, but would be posted to Headquarters in London. I was not too unhappy at this, because I felt, rightly, that I was more suited to backroom work than to frontline management. I was posted to the Economic Policy (Manpower) Division in the Department of Employment. (Over a period of ten years or so, the government department had changed from the "Ministry of Labour and National Service" to the "Ministry of Labour", then to the "Department of Employment and Productivity" under

Barbara Castle[5] and finally to the "Department of Employment" under Ted Heath's new Conservative Government.

Once again, I had to learn about a whole new world, peopled by Ministers, Private Secretaries, Senior Civil Servants, PQs (Parliamentary Questions) and Cabinet Committees.

The section I worked in was concerned with Regional Policy. The job was interesting enough, but the Department of Employment (DE) was a fringe player in policies run by the Department of Trade and Industry (DTI) and the Department of the Environment (DOE). Nevertheless, DE was represented on the relevant Cabinet Committees at both ministerial and official level. Before a Cabinet meeting or a Cabinet Committee meeting, papers were sent to ministers, who circulated them in yellow folders to officials for briefing. These were called "yellow jackets". Dealing with them was obviously a high priority. Assistant Secretaries (AS) were supposed to write the briefs, but if the AS was not available, they went down to the most senior person available, which on rare occasions was me. (Leslie Stuart, my Principal, and Derrick Dawson, my Senior Executive Officer (SEO) were senior to me.)

I had not been working in London very long, before I applied for a two-year sabbatical to work for an MSc degree in Economics. The plan was that I would then become an Economic Adviser (a double promotion). Once again, I didn't have a good interview and, in spite of a positive recommendation from Lawrie Levy, my application was turned down – with hindsight that may have been a good thing.

A few months later a competition was announced for a "class-to-class" transfer from the Executive Class to the

---

[5] Barbara Castle was a feisty left-wing Labour MP, who, as Secretary of State for Employment and Productivity, upset many of her friends on the left by producing a White Paper, entitled *In Place of Strife*, which was designed to use the law to reduce the power of trade unions.

Administrative Class. In salary terms, it involved a sideways move to a new grade called HEO(A) – 'A' for Administrative. After about two years in the grade, one was expected to be promoted to Principal, thus skipping the SEO Grade. I was nominated for this after an internal panel which included Geoffrey Holland, to whom I will refer later.

This was followed by two or three days of intensive tests, run by the Civil Service Commission. The first test was to prepare a briefing for a Minister on a proposal for a mining development in an area of natural beauty. I was very fortunate in that I had written a 'yellow jacket' briefing on a similar subject, the day before! I was then asked to chair a meeting on the same subject. I don't think I had ever chaired a meeting before, but I developed the practice of carefully working out my objectives, which I have used successfully ever since. I had to prepare arguments on two topics to present to a single interviewer. One of my topics was about 'separate development in South Africa', on which I had a different perspective from most of my competitors. In the second, I argued that the economic case for joining the European Economic Community (EEC) was not proven.

The final interview took place in a large room. The panel consisted of about twelve worthy ladies and gentlemen. At the end of the interview, the Chairman asked me if I would be interested in working for the European Commission, if the current negotiations to join the EEC were successful. I thought this might be a trick question: I was applying for a position in the British Civil Service, but could I be tempted to go and work somewhere else, soon afterwards? I replied: "I'm afraid I will have to do a Harold Wilson on this and wait and see what the terms are."[6] I had been playing golf on the North

---

[6] While Ted Heath was negotiating the UK's accession to the EEC, Harold Wilson sat on the fence, saying that he needed to see what the terms were before taking up a position.

Shore golf course at Skegness (my father, who had moved to Skegness in 1969, walked round with me) when I learned that I had been appointed as an HEO(A).

To my surprise – and slight disappointment – I stayed where I was, working on regional policy. I stayed there for nearly two years in total. As part of my training, I was required to work for Brian Martin, who was the Principal responsible for regional and local employment (and more especially unemployment) issues. Much of his section's work consisted of drafting replies to PQs about unemployment in a particular area. This was my first introduction to PQs, which, I was to discover, are part of the staple diet of Whitehall civil servants. Brian Martin was a very interesting character. He had been an army colonel and had come into the Civil Service as a Principal on retirement from the Army. He was very cultured and was more interested in having long conversations with me about French literature than answering PQs. He was also somewhat frustrated (not to say depressed) at having got stuck at Principal level, after holding such a senior position in the Army. (He was to remain at that level for a few more years, but then was promoted to Assistant Secretary and rapidly to Under-Secretary in the Health and Safety Executive (HSE)).

Lesley Stuart was also responsible for policy on Geographical Mobility. His other SEO, a Mr Clark, ran a scheme to pay allowances to workers to transfer from areas of high unemployment to work in places where there were labour shortages. In the winter of 1971/72, negotiations on the UK's entry into the EEC were well advanced. In particular, details of the UK's participation in the European Social Fund (ESF) were being worked out. The ESF was designed to promote occupational and geographical mobility. An informal meeting was arranged in Brussels to discuss this. Mr Clark didn't want to go and, as I spoke French and was an HEO(A), I was invited to go.

Our leader was Denis Sullivan, who was the AS in the recently formed Division responsible for co-ordinating DE relations with the EEC. Jack Wilde, who was an AS responsible for vocational training (i.e. occupational mobility) was the third member of the team. There was fog in Brussels, so our flight was cancelled. Denis, or his secretary, managed to get us on a flight from Southend to Ostend. The aeroplane had an enormous belly and was designed for transporting motor cars. We arrived fairly late in the evening and were met at the station in Brussels by Mike Rowe. I had been on a training course in Birmingham with Mike Rowe, some nine years earlier. This was the first time since 1966 that I had been to a French-speaking country. Mike took us to a restaurant and I remember that, after the meal, we were served brandy in enormous glasses. We stayed in the *Hotel Métropole.* At that time, it had seen better days, but the glory had faded. (Its fortunes were to be revived and, some ten years later it was taken off the UK Government list because it was too expensive!) The meetings were not memorable, but I remember thinking that I would like Mike Rowe's job, a dream that I was to realise six years later.

As an HEO(A) I was invited to go on a statistics course. I don't remember much of the detail, but some of the concepts, such as probabilities, stood me in good stead. We had a half day on computers. We were taught how to write simple programs in Basic. We were also shown a Government computer. This was housed in a room about 16 foot square. It consisted of three or four parallel banks of metal cabinets, with machinery whirring away inside them.

In June 1973, I was invited to go on a week-long visit to Bonn for HEO(A)s and Administration Trainees. This was the first such visit. The Germans laid out the red carpet for us and we suspected that they were expecting more senior staff. In spite of that, the organisation left much to be desired and there was quite a lot of delay and confusion in the arrangements. For me the highlight of the visit was an evening visit to the Bavarian House in Bonn to eat sausages and drink Bavarian beer. The host explained to us that we were in the Bavarian Embassy to the Federal German Government. The atmosphere was friendly and relaxed.

Colleagues at leisure in Koblenz

By contrast, the next evening from 6:30 to 8:00 pm we were invited to the British Minister's house for drinks. (I learned that the Minister was the number two in the Embassy.) The diplomats who were there gave the impression that they had been told they had to be there, that they were bored to be there and that they didn't want to meet these inferior beings from the Home Civil Service anyway. At one point, the Minister asked one of my colleagues in a very condescending tone:

"What exactly is an Administration Trainee?" Nevertheless, we were not in a hurry to leave. At about 8:15, one of the diplomats came round and said: "The Minister's wife expects her parties to finish *on time*!"

JIM MACKLEY

An unhappy experience

The Secretary of State for Employment (Maurice Macmillan) had a Principal Private Secretary and two Assistant Private Secretaries. The Minister of State (Robin Chichester-Clark) and the Parliamentary Under-Secretary of State (PUSS) (Dudley Smith) both had Private Secretaries. All these posts, apart from the Principal Private Secretary were at my level (HEO(A)). In the early autumn of 1972, I was in line for the next vacancy which arose. I was called over to Robin Chichester-Clark's office for an interview, which was meant to be a formality. Norman Tebbit was his Parliamentary Private Secretary. Not for the first (or last) time I fluffed the interview and Steve Loveman was appointed to the post.

A few weeks' later a vacancy arose in Maurice Macmillan's office and I was appointed as his Assistant Private Secretary, alongside Kate Jenkins. Geoffrey Holland (later Sir Geoffrey) was the Principal Private Secretary.[7] Sir Denis Barnes was the Permanent Secretary and Bernard Ingham (later Sir Bernard) was the Chief Press Officer – an important post. I had some dealings with Bernard during this period. He had been a lifelong Labour supporter. He had been brought into the Department of Employment and Productivity by Barbara Castle and retained by her Conservative successor, Robert Carr, and subsequently by Maurice Macmillan. Maurice was the son of the former Prime Minister, Harold Macmillan, and – I think it would be fair to say – he found it difficult to live up to

---

[7] A Private Secretary is a civil servant, who runs the Private Office of a Minister. In the Department of Employment the Principal Private Secretary was usually a very bright Principal in his early thirties. He was non-political. The main functions were to act as a liaison point between the Minister and the Department of Employment and the Private Offices of Ministers in other Departments.

expectations. I was scared stiff of him and I hardly spoke to him during the six weeks that I worked for him.

These were difficult times: inflation was rampant and the Government was drawing up legislation to deal with it. Maurice Macmillan was finding it difficult to cope. I was, frankly, out of my depth in this world of nuance, innuendo, intrigue and high stakes. It should have come as no surprise to me, when, late one Friday afternoon, Ian Hudson, the Director of Establishments (personnel) sent for me and told me that I was being moved to an important job on prices and incomes policy. It was, however, an almighty shock, which took me a long time to get over.

On one occasion I was told to listen in on a conversation between Maurice Macmillan and Ted Heath, the Prime Minister, who was in Paris at the time. I don't remember what it was about, but I do remember that Ted Heath was monosyllabic in his responses to the extent that at one point Macmillan asked if the Prime Minister was still there!

JIM MACKLEY

Incomes Policy and Equal Pay

In 1966 the Labour Government had introduced a prices and incomes policy – a wage freeze followed by "a period of severe restraint". This had been heavily criticised at the time by the Conservative opposition. Nevertheless, by 1972 inflation was again deemed to be getting out of control. The Conservative government needed to "do something" about inflation, but did not want to be seen to be copying the Labour Government's policies. Work began on an Inflation (Temporary Measures) Bill. On the eve of publication, the title was changed, following instructions from Ted Heath, to the Counter-Inflation (Temporary Measures) Bill. The Department of Employment and the Treasury were jointly responsible for this bill.

When I left the Private Office, I was posted to the bill team: that is the three or four person unit responsible for briefing and working on the nitty-gritty details of the bill as it passed through Parliament. The main members of the team were Alan Burridge, Assistant Secretary, Norman Mills, Principal, and my predecessor, John White, and then myself. We worked very closely with Hugh Purse in the Department's legal team. Hugh went on, some ten years later, to become "The Solicitor" in the Department of Employment. Fortunately – because my confidence was very low after my removal from Private Office – I did not have much to do on this bill, because it was enacted a few days after I transferred to the unit.

This move marked an important broadening of my expertise. Remarkably, I had worked in the Civil Service in two countries for ten years, but had very little experience of legislation. *The Employment and Training Act 1948* was the basis for most of the

Department of Employment's activities. It was couched in very general terms. The Minister of Labour and National Service was to provide: "Such facilities and services as he considers expedient for the purpose of assisting persons to select, fit themselves for, obtain and retain employment suitable to their age and capacity, of assisting employers to obtain suitable employees, and generally for the purpose of promoting employment in accordance with the requirements of the community."[8]

The *Counter-Inflation (Temporary Measures) Act 1972* was followed immediately by a more substantial Counter-Inflation Bill. For the next 16 months, I was working right at the heart of the main Government policy initiative. The Department of Employment established two Incomes Divisions under Donald Derx, who was promoted to Deputy Secretary.[9] Donald was a very dynamic 42-year old. He, along with Ted Heath and the Cabinet Secretary, William Armstrong, was the driving force behind the Incomes Policy. I was in the Division, headed by Geoffrey Brand. We were responsible for the development of policy under Denis Buckley and the development of legislation under Alan Burridge, for whom I worked. The other Division was made up of a large team, who were responsible for monitoring the implementation of the policy. Everyone was extremely busy apart from Norman Mills and me. It was decided in the early days that Alan Burridge would have an office in the Treasury, in order to speed up the reaction to parliamentary amendments to the Bill. This meant that Norman Mills and I received all the papers, but had nothing to do with them, other than read them and file them.

---

[8] Careers Services: History, Policy and Practice in the United Kingdom by David Peck.
[9] A "Division" in DE was headed by an Under-Secretary.

In September 1973, against all my expectations, I was promoted to Principal and given one of the most high-profile jobs in the Department at that level. I worked for Denis Buckley on the development of incomes policy, mainly on hours and holidays, and for Alan Burridge on equal pay for men and women.

As there was relatively full employment, employers were often looking for ways to improve pay and conditions, without breaching the incomes policy. When I was a boy, New Year's Day had been a normal working day in England, but as time passed by, more and more workers took the day off. In the autumn of 1973, it was decided to make a concession within the incomes policy, allowing employers to grant an extra day's holiday on New Year's Day. It fell to me to write to the Treasury to ask them to arrange for an order to be laid under the *Banking and Financial Dealings Act* creating a new Bank Holiday.

Sometime later, when I was no longer responsible for this policy, I went to a meeting with Michael Foot, who had taken over as Secretary of State for Employment. The meeting had been called to finalise decisions on a series of detailed matters, which needed to be resolved by the new Labour Government. Michael Foot wanted a May Day Bank Holiday. However, my former colleague in Incomes Division, Clive Tucker, explained that employers had objected to having a new Bank Holiday in mid-week, but would accept a holiday on the first Monday of May. Michael Foot accepted this argument. Thus was created the Early Spring Bank Holiday.

The Incomes Policy was controversial — to say the least — and provoked a hostile reaction from the trades unions, in particular the National Union of Mineworkers under Arthur Scargill. This led to the introduction of a 'three-day-week' decreed by the Government in order to save energy during the miners' strike and then to the calling of a General Election, which the Conservatives lost. As we were working on the policy, we were exempt from the 'three-day-week'. Indeed, Denis Buckley had a bed put in his office, though I'm not sure if he ever slept in it. During this period, I went to the Houses of Parliament on a number of occasions, usually to the House of Lords.

On one occasion I was walking through the corridors of the House of Lords with a colleague, John Dewsbury, at about 10 o'clock in the evening, when we met Lord George-Brown, who appeared to be 'in good spirits'. We were carrying our official black Government briefcases. As we passed, he said "Bureaucrats!" burst out laughing and went on his way.

Just before the General Election in February 1974, there were simultaneous debates in both Houses about the miners' strike. Norman Mills was due to be in the official box in the House of Commons and Clive Tucker was down to go to the House of Lords. Against my better judgement, Clive persuaded me to replace him, as he had a ticket for the opera. My judgement was correct and I had one of the most uncomfortable evenings of my career. Lord Gowrie, the Government spokesman, kept coming to me with questions, to which, as it was outside the matters that I was dealing with, I did not know the answers. However, I survived and the Government didn't.

When a General Election is called, the Civil Service produces a number of papers setting out policy options for each of the parties or combination of parties, which might form the next Government. This was the first occasion when I had been involved in this process. As the probable outcome was uncertain, the different policy options took on added significance.

In the event there was a "Hung Parliament" and the Labour Party under Harold Wilson formed a minority Government. Developments in my area were of particular interest, because the Labour Party had been opposed to the prices and incomes policy. When they came to power, they obviously had to "do something". I recall one incident that illustrates the flexibility of senior civil servants. As I have said, Donald Derx was one of the main architects of the Conservative Government's policy. Shortly after the election, however, he wrote a speech for Michael Foot, the new Secretary of State, criticising "the arid rigidities of incomes policy".

One of the last achievements of the Labour Government in 1970 had been the enactment of the *Equal Pay Act 1970*. This provided, *inter alia,* that it would be unlawful for employers to pay less to a woman than they would to a man doing "the same, or broadly similar work" after the act came into force on 29 December 1975. I first came across the legislation in my early dealings with incomes policy, because some employers and trade unions sought to justify dubious pay increases, as necessary in order to comply with the incomes policy. Part of my job over the next three years was to work with my colleagues monitoring the incomes policy to ensure that the policy was being interpreted correctly with regard to equal pay.

Towards the end of 1973, the Conservative Government decided that it wanted to introduce legislation on Sex Discrimination. One day, my future colleague and friend, Bob David, telephoned me. He introduced himself and said he had been appointed to lead the team on the Sex Discrimination Bill, which would have implications for the Equal Pay Act. His immediate question was: did I want the Equal Pay legislation to apply to oil rigs? At the time, I thought the question was absurd, but it was indicative of the thorough approach that was taken to the drafting of legislation at that time.

After the first election in 1974, the new Labour Government decided it wanted more substantial legislation on sex discrimination. The Home Office, under Roy Jenkins, was in the lead, but the Department of Employment had a very important role to play. I was transferred from the Incomes Policy Division to work solely on equal pay. Dorothy Kent was the Under-Secretary in charge of that and a myriad of other policy areas. Bryan Winkett headed up a new Branch with three Principals. Eve Craske was in charge of Women's Employment Policy, Bob David headed the bill team and I was in charge of Equal Pay.

As an aside we were housed in a magnificent building: number 32 St. James' Square. It was said that, at one time, it had been the Bishop of London's Palace. It had magnificent toilets and Bryan Winkett had a palatial office and the Department's Solicitor had a better one. Eve Craske and I, however, had offices in the servants' quarters: there was an (unused) service lift for food and crockery. My office overlooked the well and, until recently, it had been used as a carpenter's workshop. Nevertheless, I spent one of the most enjoyable periods of my career working in that office.

My main job was to ensure that the Government was seen to be doing its best to ensure that the *Equal Pay Act* was implemented correctly and on time. In fact, the Government had very little power under the legislation. (The Act gave rights to employees, which were enforceable in Industrial Tribunals (civil courts dealing solely with employment matters).) (Ironically, some ten years later, Eve Craske was the Secretary of the Industrial Tribunals (i.e. she ran them) while I was responsible for policy on the tribunals.)

This was a good job. It was important enough to have a Principal in charge (me), but not important enough to attract much attention from my superiors. Consequently, for much of the work I dealt directly with ministers. It was my job to explain the issues to successive ministers (usually Parliamentary Under Secretaries of State) and the approach we were taking to these issues. This was particularly important when there was a change of Minister. During this period, I told myself, no doubt with a little *hubris*, that Government policy on Equal Pay was what I said it was.

This was far from being the case with regard to the Sex Discrimination Bill. I was astonished at the intensity of the debates and discussions within the Civil Service that went into the detailed preparation of the bill. Anthony Lester QC, who was an adviser to Roy Jenkins, also had an important input.

The first stage was the preparation of Instructions to Counsel: the detailed policy objectives of the proposed legislation. I have already mentioned an early discussion about whether the law should apply to offshore installations – the territorial scope of the legislation. There was a more important discussion about the breadth of scope of the legislation. Everyone was agreed that it should apply to discrimination between men and women. But it was for debate – and hotly debated – whether it should also be unlawful to discriminate on grounds of marriage and on grounds of pregnancy. Dorothy Kent had a rigorous intellectual approach to the legislation, which let her down on one occasion. In a room full of mostly men, she stood up and said: "Pregnancy has absolutely nothing to do with sex!"

I had a great admiration for Dorothy Kent and generally got on well with her. She had a powerful, quite shrill voice. Her office was in number 8 St. James's Square – near to the Ministers – and across the square from me. Quite often she would ring me up, though I sometimes thought she didn't need a phone to make herself heard. She would begin "Mr Mackley…" followed by a short, ominous pause. She would then launch into a long tirade about something which she thought was not quite right. My response usually was: "Perhaps I should come over and talk to you about it", which she usually accepted. This gave her time to calm down and me time to think what I was going to say.

My involvement in the development of the legislation concerned the relationship between the *Equal Pay Act* and the Sex Discrimination Bill.

After the Instructions to Counsel had been agreed by officials and then by Ministers, they were sent to the Parliamentary Draftsman, whose job was to turn the instructions into a draft bill. This draft was again hotly debated by officials and amendments requested. Then the Bill was published and the parliamentary process began. The process was the same as for the Counter-Inflation Bills, but I was much more closely involved on this occasion. Draft amendments were tabled by MPs and officials had a few hours in which to advise Ministers how to respond. There was not, in fact, much opposition from the Conservatives, who had been going to propose a similar bill, but there was considerable opposition from a group of four Labour MPs, led by Renée Short, who thought the bill was too weak.

The main policy issue, as far as I was concerned, was whether the *Equal Pay Act* should be repealed and incorporated into the Sex Discrimination Bill. Most of the people involved with the bill favoured the latter course, including my immediate boss, Bryan Winkett. I argued, almost alone, that the *Equal Pay Act* was a complex piece of legislation, which had been agreed by Parliament after lengthy debate, where a compromise had been reached between those who had wanted tougher legislation and many employers, who considered legislation to be inappropriate. Now was not the time to reopen the 'can of worms', before the legislation had come into force. The counter-argument was that pay was the most important element in discrimination and it was absurd not to incorporate it into the new bill. This debate raged for some months within the Civil Service, though I don't remember it being raised in Parliament. At the end of the day, my line prevailed, partly following the intervention of John Locke, who had been the Under Secretary in charge of the original Equal Pay Bill, but, who was now a Deputy Secretary with responsibilities unconnected with the Sex Discrimination Bill. John Locke was unconventional for a civil servant at that time. He had long hair – well before that became fashionable in men – and wore casual clothes and suede shoes. He had a relaxed style, but the sharpest mind, that I ever came across and a sharp tongue to go with it, whenever the occasion arose.

Soon after I first took over the equal pay responsibility the European Commission invited 'experts' from the three new Member States (Denmark, Ireland and the UK to a meeting to discuss a possible European Economic Community (EEC) Directive on equal pay. I went from the UK, in spite of the fact that I knew hardly anything about the subject. I remember receiving detailed (and quite aggressive) briefing from a senior statistician, a Mr Turner, explaining the difference between 'wages' and 'earnings', a distinction, which can easily be overlooked in discussions about pay, but which I never forgot.

Some months later the Commission made a proposal for a Council Directive on Equal Pay for men and women. This was the first occasion that the Department of Employment had been involved in the process of negotiating EEC legislation and I was at the heart of it – though perhaps not quite as much at the heart of it as I would have been, if Bryan Winkett had not decided to go himself to the Council meetings. It was my job, however, to provide him and the United Kingdom Permanent Representation to the European Communities (UKREP) with detailed briefing. As there were few precedents, I had to invent the form that the briefing would take. (Throughout my career I preferred to work from first principles (others would say to reinvent the wheel) rather than to follow an established formula.) I worked hard on this briefing, often late into the evening.

As well as briefing for the meetings in Brussels, I also had to go to one or two meetings with the House of Lords Scrutiny Committee, which had been set up to examine the Government's negotiating stance on EEC legislative proposals. There was also a House of Commons Scrutiny Committee, but I don't recall being summoned to meet them. I also became one of the few people in the world to understand the relationship between Gibraltar, Guernsey and Jersey and the EEC, although I am not sure that I can still explain it 45 years later! These territories were not part of the EEC, but they were required to comply with EEC legislation. I therefore had to write to the authorities in these three dependencies to enquire what steps they were taking to comply with the new Directive, when it was adopted. For some reason, which I can't explain, the Directive did not apply to the Isle of Man.

A contentious issue in relation to equal pay, both in the context of the original Equal Pay Bill and the proposal for an EEC Directive was the definition of 'equal work'. In 1951 the International Labour Organisation (ILO) had adopted a Convention (100) on equal remuneration. This provided for equal pay for 'work of equal value'. The *Equal Pay Act* had used the formula equal pay for the 'same or broadly similar work or *work to which an equal value has been attributed under a job evaluation scheme'*. So, for example, office workers and factory workers could not be compared, unless there had been a formal job evaluation scheme. This definition became central in the discussions in Brussels. That situation was even more confused, because the Treaty of Rome (Article 119) referred in English to equal pay 'for equal work', whereas in French it was *pour un même travail* and I believe in Danish *samme arbejde*.[10] As all languages are equal under EEC law, this gave the lawyers plenty to argue about.

In the negotiations, the argument boiled down to one or two words: 'work to which an equal value *has been* attributed' favoured by Bryan Wnkett (correctly, if the *Equal Pay Act* was going to meet the requirements of the Directive without amendment) and 'work to which an equal value *is* attributed', favoured by most people in Brussels, including John Rimington, who was the Counsellor in UKREP responsible for leading the UK negotiating team. When the Directive came for a decision in the Council of Ministers, John Grant, the UK minister found himself in a difficult position. The Labour Government was not very 'pro-EEC', but he did not want to find himself blocking European legislation on equal pay. Council Directive 75/117/EEC was adopted on 10 February 1975 with the formula 'work to which an equal value *is* attributed'.

A similar issue was raised by a Belgian air-hostess, Gabrielle Defrenne, who took a whole series of discrimination cases against her employers, SABENA, the Belgian national airline, to the European Court of Justice (ECJ). These cases rested on

---

[10] The words *même* and *samme* can be translated into English as *same* and are therefore, arguably, narrower in scope than the English definition of *equal* in the Equal Pay Act 1970.

the interpretation of Article 119 of the Treaty of Rome and whether the article was 'directly applicable' in the Member States. The argument was that as the Treaty required equal pay for equal work, workers had a right to equal pay without the need for further legislation either at European or national level. The important thing for the UK would be that, if she was completely successful, women in the UK would have a right to claim retrospectively from the date the UK joined the EEC, that is from 1 January 1973, whereas the *Equal Pay Act* was only due to come into force on 29 December 1975.

I remember doing detailed, but probably not very sophisticated, calculations of the potential cost to UK employers. I estimated these to be about £1 billion, the equivalent of the whole cost of the Concorde project or the Channel Tunnel project, both of which were being debated at the time and both of which were considered to be prohibitively expensive for Governments to undertake. In a landmark Judgment, the ECJ held that article 119 of the Treaty of the European Community was of such a character as to have horizontal direct effect, and therefore enforceable not merely between individuals and the government, but also between private parties. I think there might have been something in the Judgment, which made it non-retrospective. In any case, I don't remember the Judgment having huge cost implications for UK employers.

The *Equal Pay Act* also required the removal of discriminatory references to men and women from 'collective agreements'. As the deadline for implementation of the legislation approached, Ministers became increasingly anxious about whether this provision was being complied with. I was instructed to find out. For this I was allowed to recruit a Senior Executive Officer to do the research. The task proved to be more difficult than anyone had imagined. The Department of Employment published a book on rates of pay, hours and holidays each year, giving information for some 200 collective agreements and Wages Councils. The Wages Council information was easy to find, because that was published in Statutory Instruments. We asked the people responsible for the collective agreements to provide us with copies of them. In some cases this was straightforward, but most of the agreements had been concluded decades before, with only the amendments, mainly to rates of pay, being agreed each year. In some cases, they were unable to find them. Nevertheless, the exercise fulfilled the policy objective which was to make sure that no collective agreements were discriminatory.

As the deadline approached, it was also decided to launch a publicity campaign to remind employers of their obligations and employees of their rights under the legislation. I had a budget of £100,000 for this purpose. I immediately thought of a television advertising campaign, but I was quickly told that – even then in 1975 - £100,000 would buy only a few minutes of TV advertisements. Instead, with the help of the Department's Press Office and an outside agency, we produced a series of press adverts, for publication in the national press, which I was quite pleased with.

On 29th December 1975, Michael Foot made a Ministerial Broadcast on television to remind employers and employees that the Act was coming into force. I wrote the text of that broadcast. Michael Foot was a great public speaker and he read my speech beautifully. However, towards the end I had written something which was not grammatically coherent and Michael Foot stumbled over it. I doubt if anyone else noticed it, but I did.

In the spring of 1974, the International Labour Organisation (ILO) invited me to attend a symposium for European 'experts' on the application of ILO Convention 100 on equal remuneration. This was held at the beautiful ILO headquarters on the banks of Lake Geneva.

ILO Building, Geneva, 1974

I was joined at the colloquium by Marie Patterson, who was to be President of the Trades Union Congress (TUC) in 1975. As I was still very new to the subject (and she wasn't!) she was very helpful. Experts from the Union of Soviet Socialist Republics (USSR) were also present. This was the first (and only) time I came into close contact with officials from the USSR. The meeting had an agenda with one or two items for discussion each day. Each expert was invited to speak about the item on the agenda. On the first day, the Soviet expert said nothing. The following day different points were for discussion. However, when invited to speak, the Soviet expert spoke at length on the subjects that had been for discussion the previous day: by that time, she had received her instructions from Moscow as to what to say! This pattern continued throughout the first six days of the Colloquium.

There was then a break of a couple of days, while selected experts (not including me) drafted the report of the Colloquium. On one of these days I went with Marie on a train to visit Chamonix and the nearby tourist attraction of *la mer de glace*, a valley glacier located on the northern slopes of the Mont Blanc massif.

L'Aiguille du Midi

One consequence of the successive pay policies was that public sector pay was frozen or increases were kept at a low level for a number of years. Then there was a review and we were given a massive pay increase. With my promotion, my salary doubled between 1973 and 1975. In order to celebrate the pay increase, Bob David, who was brought up in India, suggested that we go with our spouses to *Veeraswamy's* a posh Indian restaurant on Regent Street. Guided by Bob's expertise we had a fabulous meal in a wonderful setting. However, the bill for the six of us was £45. So our share of £15 was equivalent to one week's housekeeping money!

A pleasant interlude

In the autumn of 1976, I was invited to go on a six-week course at the prestigious *Ecole Nationale d'Administration* (ENA) in Paris. This is the post-graduate *Grande Ecole*, which most future French Ministers, senior civil servants and heads of nationalised industries go to, including, for example, François Hollande (at about the same time as me) and, 27 years later, Emmanuel Macron. This gave me a wonderful insight into the working of the French Government system. I also met two men, Syd Allman and Brian Smith, with whom, along with their wives, Wendy and Joan, we have been friendly ever since. I also met Barney Smith, from the Foreign Office, with whom I was to work closely in 1990.

At the time I was also friendly with Alyson Bailes. She had a formidable intellect. As part of the hospitality offered by the French, we were all invited to dinner with a senior *énarque*, i.e. a graduate of ENA. Alyson and I were invited by a senior person in the nationalised gas industry. It was a very civilised evening, but I remember at one point our host turning to Alyson, either in frustration or amusement, and saying: *Dites-moi, Alyson, vous qui savez tout....* (*Tell me, Alyson, you who know everything...*) I bumped into Alyson some years later in Brussels. At that time, she was working in the UK Embassy to the Netherlands. A short time before, she had been in a car with her ambassador, when he had been shot and killed by the Irish Republican Army (IRA). Alyson said she had protected herself with her handbag. As a sad corollary to that story, it was said that the Ambassador's wife, having lost her husband, was given very short notice to leave her house in The Hague. The Foreign Office could be ruthless on occasions. Following a distinguished career in the Foreign

Office and other international organisations, Alyson was H.M. Ambassador to Finland from 2000 to 2002.

While we were on the course we had French language lessons. One day the tutor of my group (the top group) played a tape recording of a traffic accident at a crossroads on the *Boulevard de Raspail.* We were told to go away and write about what we had heard. We could write in "proper" French or in slang. Sixteen years previously I had spent a year at the *lycée* at Pontarlier, where I spent most of my time mixing with students and young teachers. I decided to write in slang. It's not all that difficult: bad language anywhere tends to be very repetitive. Any way my report received fulsome praise at the next full meeting of the course. It was returned to me with compliments and a few corrections, including one phrase which I had spelt correctly, but which the tutor had thought should have been spelt differently.[11]

The course included a week away from Paris studying the French regional and local Government set-up. We were the lucky ones: we were sent to the South of France. We spent the first two days in Marseilles, which was the seat of the regional *Préfecture.* We had a session with Gaston Deferre. We got our photo in the local paper and I got a mention for asking a question. I asked M. Deferre whether he was going to be a candidate in the next French Presidential elections. His answer was, of course, non-committal. He was a candidate, but he didn't win.

We were invited one evening to the British Consul's house for drinks. That was not a pleasant experience. All I remember about it was an "old" woman expatriate earwigging me about

---

[11] There is quite a strong expletive which sounds like *vain Dieu* and which I had always assumed was spelt that way and meant "vain God". That is what my tutor thought too. However, some years before I had seen the expression used in a novel by Georges Bernanos, where it is spelt *vingt dieux*. That was the spelling I used.

the terrible Labour Government and the awful tax system. Subsequently we lived abroad for fifteen years, but, on the basis of that experience, I always tried to avoid one-to-one contact with elderly female expatriates.

After Marseilles we went to Toulon, which is the *Préfecture* of the Var *Département*. It is also one of the main navy bases. I spent my 47th birthday there. Brian Smith took me out for lunch. In the afternoon I dreamt that we were sitting in a warm room and a man was talking to us about the French naval defences. I dreamt that Brian was also sleeping.

From there we went to La Londe les Maures a smallish town in the Var. We spent most of the day with the mayor. It was customary for one of our number to give a thankyou speech at the end of each session. On this occasion Syd Allman had been designated to do it. Syd was not the best French speaker in the group, but he was not as bad as he made out. He started off by saying that he spoke French *comme une vache espagnole* (like a Spanish cow) and proceeded to lace his talk with a number of deliberate mistakes and malapropisms. (He came from the Department of Stealth and Total Obscurity.)

On the Saturday I went to St Tropez for the first time. The Friday had been a glorious day, but the Saturday was a grey November day. I have been back there twice since then. The first time was in August 1979 and St Tropez was at its glorious best: I have never been anywhere where the sea has been a deeper blue. The last time I went there was in the early nineties. Our son, Peter, was living and working on a campsite near Antibes. We went to stay on the campsite over Christmas. On the Thursday after Christmas we decided to go to St Tropez for the day. There was a two-kilometre traffic jam to get into the town - on the 28th or 29th December!

A less pleasant experience

I realised when I went on the ENA course that I was "burning my boats". I was leaving my job on equal pay and I would be at the mercy of the Establishments people when I came back. Nevertheless, things had improved since I first joined and I did expect to have a say. By this time, parts of the Department of Employment had been hived off to agencies. There were six possibilities: DE proper; ACAS (the Advisory Conciliation and Arbitration Service); Manpower Services Commission (MSC) head office; the Training Services Agency; the Employment Services Agency (ESA); and the Health and Safety Executive (HSE). The ESA was my fifth choice. I also expressed a preference for economic policy over social policy. The job I was offered was as Operations Manager with functional responsibility for the DRO (Disablement Resettlement Officer) service. I resisted this, but was told that the alternative was an obscure backroom job in Establishments or Finance. Before I accepted the job I asked for it to be noted that if ever the job in the UKREP in Brussels came up, I wished to be considered. There was also a better job in the same Branch of ESA, dealing with policy on Disabled People, which I said I would be interested in, if ever it came along.

The Operations Manager job was a good job: it was just one that I didn't want and for which I was not particularly well suited. The MSC was a relatively new organisation. It was based on a more "modern", brash, go-getting, results-orientated philosophy. It embraced all the latest management planning ideas. Thus there was an MSC Strategic Plan and an ESA Strategic Plan; there was also an MSC Operational Plan and an ESA Operational Plan. There were also personal development plans and there may also have been a specific plan for the employment of disabled people. (I may have got some of the titles wrong, but not the numbers!) I found all this terribly frustrating. (It is upsetting me to write about it forty years later!) At one point I was asked to say what were the constraints on achieving our objectives and I said that we spent so much time drawing up plans that we didn't have time to do the things we were supposed to be doing.

Nevertheless, I did the job for about six months. It brought me back to the real world of Local Offices, which I had left eight years previously. (It seemed like a lifetime away!) Each month I had to go to Leeds to star in the final session of a DRO training course. I also visited Portland College near Mansfield and I went to a Conference at Weston-Super-Mare, which was a pleasant experience. It was also while I was working on this job that Nottingham Forest got promoted to the First Division!

After I had been there for about six months, Stanley Tolson, my boss, asked me if I was still interested in the policy job and if I was still interested in the UKREP job, both of which, he said, were possibly on offer. I replied "Yes" to both. This put him in a dilemma, because the policy job was coming up and he didn't really want to give it to me, if he was going to have to find someone else in a few months' time. To his credit, he did give it to me. This was a much better job for me. It was a traditional policy job, and, in addition, I was Secretary of the National Advisory Council on the Employment of Disabled People (NACEDP). This was a relatively high-powered body chaired by Geoffrey Gilbertson (later Sir Geoffrey) who rode around in a wheel-chair. Its members included John Edmonds, who at the time was an up-and-coming figure in the National Union of General and Municipal Workers.

The policy part of the job included advising ministers on policy. The Minister (PUSS) I dealt with was John Grant, who had been the same Minister as I had dealt with before when working on equal pay and with whom I had a good relationship. This was a busy job and we did a lot of briefing for ministers. I had an SEO (John Grubb) and an HEO(A), first Helen Leiser and then Kate Walker.

One week we were asked to prepare some briefing for another DE Minister, who was going to his constituency in Stoke-on-Trent at the weekend. He was going to talk about employment of disabled people. He sent for me on the Friday morning to talk to him about the briefing we had provided. Someone else had written the briefing, but I had signed it off. So it was no excuse when the minister told me, in no uncertain terms, that it was not very good, because it wasn't. He had written out what he proposed to say instead. This was the sort of ideological nonsense that politicians produce in opposition, but most definitely was not Government policy. I asked him if he had spoken to John Grant about it and he said he hadn't. The minister concerned, whose name, fortunately, I can't remember, had a reputation for being a difficult and unpleasant man to deal with. My experience during this discussion did nothing to contradict that reputation. I held my ground and the outcome was that I was given a few hours to rewrite his speech, which I did.

I also had a "run-in" with Alf Morris, who was Minister for the Disabled in the Department for Health and Social Security (DHSS). At the time three-wheel Reliant cars were available for disabled people to get to work. Alf Morris wanted to introduce what came to be known as the Motability Scheme. For reasons that I can no longer remember the ESA was opposed to this. We had a meeting with Alf Morris, where I got in an argument with him and, much to the surprise and delight of Stanley Tolson, seemed to get the better of him. We won the battle, but not the war: the Motability Scheme was introduced and is still going strong, whereas the three-wheeler Reliant Robin cars are a dim and distant – and largely unlamented – memory.

I also came into contact with the Honours system (for knighthoods, MBE, etc.) Many of the members of NACEDP were in the running for Honours and files came across my desk asking for recommendations.

I was also a member of an advisory committee set up by Dr Vidali in the European Commission in Luxembourg on the Rehabilitation of Disabled People. Managers of rehabilitation establishments were also on the Committee. I have to confess that I don't remember very much about what we talked about at these meetings and I would be hard-pressed, then and now, to justify the expenditure involved. I had never been to Luxembourg before, but I soon discovered, of course, that it is a beautiful city.

I did have some interesting journeys. I usually travelled by Luxair (the Luxembourg national airline) from Heathrow to Luxembourg. On one occasion our flight home was delayed. We sat in the hotel in Luxembourg city centre until we heard that the plane was ready for boarding. When we got there the plane was full and five or six of us were unable to board. By this time the airport was almost deserted. I managed to find someone, and after a long and acrimonious discussion I persuaded them to provide us with a taxi to a hotel with evening meal and breakfast and a taxi back to the airport for the plane the next morning!

The last meeting of this group I was due to attend was arranged for the morning following a full-day NACEDP meeting. I obviously had to attend the NACEDP meeting, but I wanted to go to the meeting in Luxembourg, as well. I was still young – 38. I decided that I could attend the meeting in London, get a plane to Brussels and then get a train to Luxembourg arriving in time to get some hours' sleep in the hotel I normally stayed in which was near the railway station.

I booked my tickets and duly arrived at Heathrow airport and into the departure lounge on time. I even telephoned Jennifer to say that, so far, everything was on schedule. The reason for my concern was that there was a strike or go-slow somewhere in the system. The flight finally took off round about 10:00 pm and arrived in Brussels around midnight, local time. Having missed the last train, I had no idea how I was going to get to Luxembourg, other than the vague thought of hiring a car. After the plane had landed, a man boarded the aircraft and announced that if anyone had difficulties getting to their final destination, they were to go and see him in the airport. I did so and he said, straightaway: we'll get a taxi!

Some considerable time later, a young chap came to me and told me he was to take me to Luxembourg. It transpired that he was a student and the taxi belonged to his girlfriend's father. I got in the taxi. He asked me if I minded if he stopped for fuel. I replied that, if he was short of fuel, that seemed like a good idea. We spent the next 20 minutes or so driving up and down the Brussels ring road looking for a petrol station that was open. With the possibility of hiring a car in mind, I had already looked at the route and decided the best route was via Namur, Bastogne and Arlon. I was somewhat surprised, therefore, when he set off on the route for Liège. I asked him if he knew the route and he said that he did. The result was that we did two sides of a triangle to get to Namur (about 160 km instead of 65). I was tired and very hungry. I asked him if we could stop somewhere to get something to eat. He didn't find anywhere until we had crossed the Luxembourg border. There we stopped at one of several brightly illuminated establishments and I ordered a beer and a sandwich. I was served by a well-proportioned, lightly-clad young woman, who seemed somewhat disappointed when I replied in the negative to her offer of further services. When I arrived at my hotel it was closed for the night, but I eventually roused someone and went to bed at about 3:30 a.m.

About nine years later, I had similar travel problems. I was a member of a Council of Europe "expert" working group on employment aspects of data protection. The group met at the Council of Europe's Headquarters in Strasbourg. Towards the end of one meeting, I discovered that my flight back to London had been cancelled. Jennifer was supposed to be meeting me at Heathrow. This was at a time before mobile phones were in common use. Jennifer was the Librarian at St Helen's School in Northwood. I managed to get a message to her to say that my flight had been cancelled.

With my Luxembourg experience in mind, I decided to get a train to Brussels and get a flight from Brussels to London. I managed to send another message to this effect to Jennifer, via the school office. Two major potential pitfalls were only narrowly avoided. The first one was that I had read the train timetable the wrong way round – across instead of down (or down instead of across). The result was that the train journey took an hour and a half longer than I had calculated – when the train pulled into Luxembourg station, according to my calculation it should already have been near Brussels. I decided to jump off the train at the station in Brussels called Brussels Luxembourg and get a taxi to the airport. Fortunately at that time the security checks were not as stringent as they are now and I was able to catch my plane by the skin of my teeth.

In my conversation with the secretary of the school, I had said only casually that the plane from Brussels was flying into

Gatwick airport, which is 47 miles from Heathrow and about 45 miles further from Watford, where we lived. Jennifer had a long discussion with the secretary as to whether I had really said Gatwick. She would not have been amused if she'd gone to the wrong airport or indeed if she had gone all the way to Gatwick and I had missed the plane!

On another occasion Jennifer dropped me off at Heathrow and I gave her strict instructions to pick me up at exactly the same place when I came back. On the appointed day I went out of the arrival area and crossed the road to where I was supposed to be meeting Jennifer – or so I thought. I waited around for about an hour, but there was still no sign of her - and no mobile phones either. I don't want to raise Jennifer's ire even now by asking her what the exact outcome was – we are still married! – but she had also been waiting an hour in the place where she had dropped me, which was just across the road from the **departure** area.

Brussels 1

After a long period of negotiation and uncertainty, I was posted to the UKREP in Brussels at the end of February 1978. This was the job I really wanted. Syd Allman and I were candidates for the same job. In the end they gave me the job and Syd a different job – on Regional Policy. He worked in the next office. My title was First Secretary (Social Affairs). My boss (Counsellor (AS) level) was Gerry Wilson from the Scottish Office, who had taken over from John Rimington, from the Department of Employment, in the previous autumn.

This was a complete new world. As well as living in a different country, I had to get to know the workings of a British Overseas Representation (and the Foreign Office) and of the European institutions. To start with the Representation. The Ambassador was Sir Donald Maitland, an ambassador of the old school, with a fine mind, a strict, but fair, office manager, who ran a 'tight ship'. His deputy, Bill Nicholl, later Sir William Nicholl, was a very different character.[12] Both were Scots. Bill was very colourful, also with a powerful intellect, but a trenchant wit, which sometimes got him into trouble. Bill was Gerry Wilson's boss and the senior person I had most to do with.

Every Monday morning at 9:15, almost without exception, the Ambassador held a meeting of all diplomatic staff (Second Secretary and above). Attendance was compulsory, as was punctuality. Every other day of the week, I could leave my house in Overijse, about 12 km away, after the rush hour at about 8:55 and arrive at the office well before 9:30, but on Monday mornings I needed to leave at 8:30.

---

[12] Sadly, while I was writing this chapter, I learned that Sir William Nicholl had died recently (March 2016).

Many of my colleagues at that time went on to greater things. Several went on to be ambassadors, including (Sir) Roderick Braithwaite (Moscow) and (Sir) Christopher Meyer (Washington). (Sir) John Coles went to London as Margaret Thatcher's Foreign Policy Adviser. He was succeeded in UKREP and later in Margaret Thatcher's office by Charles Powell later to become Lord Powell. John Mogg was a fellow First Secretary for most of the time I was there. He went on to be a Director-General in the European Commission and later, as Lord Mogg, Chairman of OFGEM[13] and then of the EU Energy Regulators. Some years later, in the mid-80s, there was a major Cabinet row involving Michael Heseltine and Leon Brittan – the 'Westland Affair'. The civil servants involved included John Mogg and Bernard Ingham, whom I had known when he was Press Officer in the Department of Employment and who was the Prime Minister's Press Officer at the time of the Westland Affair. Bernard Ingham, too, had an interesting career: Barbara Castle brought him into the Department of Employment and Productivity in 1968 and he ended up as the very influential Spokesman for Mrs Thatcher.

In those days before faxes, emails and mobile phones, communication with London was by telegram and Diplomatic Bag, though we were connected to the internal Whitehall phone network. It was an office rule that a telegram was sent to London, reporting on all Council meetings, including the Committee of Permanent Representatives (COREPER) and Working Groups, on the same day as the meeting. This meant that, in my case, most Tuesday and Wednesday evenings and some Thursdays, I worked until 8:00 pm. As none of us could type, secretaries stayed behind as well to take dictation or copy typing.

---

[13] The UK electricity and gas market regulator.

The principal function of the office was to represent the United Kingdom at meetings within the framework of the Council of Ministers. In my case this was the Social Questions Working Group. This group met most Tuesdays and Wednesdays from 10:00 am to 6:00 pm, with a strict two hour break for lunch. In my innocence, I had expected the Commission representative to be in the chair and the proceedings to be conducted in French.

Gerry Wilson took me to the first meeting and introduced me to the Danish Chairman, Morten Fenger. As it happened he did speak French – his wife was French. Interpretation was available in all the languages of the nine Member States – Danish, Dutch, English, French, German and Italian – though there was a shortage of Danish interpreters. The Council Secretariat team was led by Enzo Chioccioli, an Italian with a very quick and inventive intellect, for whom I developed a strong admiration and later a personal friendship. He and most of his team spoke French at the meetings.

The other countries were represented as follows. Jean Gillet was the Belgian. Otto Dibelius was the German. His grandfather, also called Otto Dibelius, was a senior Lutheran bishop, who had had a delicate and difficult relationship with Hitler during the war. Otto's father had had a good war: he was sent to Norway at the beginning and stayed there until the end. Otto's assistant was Dieter Kaschke, with whom I became good friends outside the office, along with his wife Birgit. They came back to Brussels in the nineties and we are still in contact with them. Birgit is an interesting character: she speaks English and French very quickly and with considerable fluency, but tends to forget which language she is supposed to be speaking. So, she would ring us up and speak to me in French and then ask to speak to Jennifer and rattle on in German to her, even though she knew Jennifer didn't speak German.

The French representative was Maurice Ramond. Though a product of a *Grande Ecole*, Maurice was not a typical smooth French diplomat, which is probably why I liked him. He had strong Gaullist convictions, which he summarised for me as being a sense of order and tradition with a strong social conscience. In meetings, we were often arguing against each other, but outside the meetings we were good colleagues, as indeed were all members of the group. We still exchange letters once a year and we went to see him last time we were in Paris.

Ireland was represented by Pascal Leonard. I had quite a lot of dealings with him, because, with our common history and language, we often faced common challenges in relation to Commission proposals. The Italian team was led by Signor Cristofanelli, a very senior diplomat with an aristocratic pedigree. There were two other members of his team, who came to the group meetings. I can't now remember the name of the number two at the beginning, but some years later, it was a young diplomat called di Medici – his wife insisted that the emphasis was on the 'e'. He had previously been Italian Consul in one of the German speaking Swiss cantons. He did not like the Swiss, whom he described as 'a nation of policemen'. It was only the junior Italian representative Signor di Stefano, who came from the Ministry of Labour. He complained to me during the British Presidency that I didn't let him speak very much. That was probably true, because he had a tendency to talk for a long time without saying very much.

The Luxembourg representative was Monsieur Schintgen. He was also the senior civil servant in the Luxembourg Ministry of Labour and so he did not attend all the meetings. On one occasion, some years later – probably during the UK Presidency in 1981 – I tried to telephone him in his office. The telephone operator said that M. Schintgen was out and that he, the telephone operator, was the only person in the office. I reflected at that time how much easier Schintgen's job was than mine. Typically in the UK we had to consult three or four Ministries and two or three Branches of the Department of Employment before establishing our negotiating position. M. Schintgen, on the other hand, only had to consult his Minister, Jacques Santer, who was also Minister of Finance, and possibly the Ministry of Foreign Affairs. I met Jacques Santer in London in 1981. He was a very nice man, who later became President of the European Commission.

The Dutch representative was Erik van Traa. He was the *doyen*, the senior member of the group and, because of that and his strong personality, very influential. He was also somewhat eccentric. He always spoke (bad) French in the group meetings. He organised regular lunches for the members of the group – at the *Auberge Fleurie,* an old-fashioned French-Belgian restaurant about 300 metres from the Council building – and gave a lavish buffet at his apartment once a year in May or June. On at least two occasions it was very hot, with the thermometer on a nearby building registering 34 degrees at 8:00 pm. I kept in touch with Erik and went to see him in 2005 in Athens, to where he had retired, but received a message the following year to say that he had died.

The function of the Social Questions Working Group was to prepare legislation and other documents for the Labour and Social Affairs Council of Ministers, on which the UK was represented by a Minister from the Department of Employment. As the Labour Government in those days did not attach much importance to European matters, the UK was usually represented by John Grant, who was Parliamentary Under-Secretary of State (PUSS) in the Department of Employment under Michael Foot and later Albert Booth.

The procedure was that the Commission made a proposal for legislation, typically for a Council Directive, which, when adopted by the Council of Ministers, was legally binding in all Member States. This proposal was sent at the same time to the Council of Ministers, the European Parliament and a body called the Economic and Social Committee, consisting of representatives of employers and workers. The latter two bodies were asked for their Opinions, but, in those days, it was the Council of Ministers alone who took the final decision, generally only paying lip service to the Opinions of the other two bodies. So, the Social Questions Working Group was a very powerful body. We debated the Commission's proposals line by line and word by word. The unstated aim was to reach agreement on the main body of the text, leaving half a dozen items for agreement at a higher level.

Normally, the Labour and Social Affairs Council met towards the end of each six-month Presidency.[14] (In those days, each Member State held the Presidency of the Council of Ministers for six months in strict alphabetical order of the name of the country in its own language. Representatives of that country chaired all the meetings within the framework of the Council of Ministers.) So, around the middle of May and November, the Social Questions Working Group sent a report to the COREPER. There were in fact two COREPERs. The first was attended by Ambassadors, in our case by Sir Donald Maitland, and dealt with Foreign Affairs, External Trade and all matters concerned with relations with countries who were not members of the European Economic Community (EEC). The second

---

[14] The title of the meeting had traditionally been the "Social Affairs" Council. John Grant boasted that, before my time, he had got the title changed to "Labour and Social Affairs". Under pressure from the Conservatives, the title was changed later to "Employment and Social Affairs".

COREPER dealt with matters relating to the internal market and was attended by the Deputy Permanent Representatives, in our case by Bill Nicholl. Each format of COREPER usually met for a whole day every week, the Ambassadors on a Wednesday and the Deputies on a Thursday. Both these meetings always had long agendas and often went on late into the evening. In my case the item was called "Preparation for the Labour and Social Affairs Council". When our item was due to be debated, Gerry Wilson and I were summoned by Bill Nicholl's assistant, Nicole Mingins, to go over to the Council building to sit alongside Bill and advise him during the discussion – having previously given him a written and oral briefing. COREPER would typically reach agreement on two or three points on each item under discussion, leaving the most difficult points for discussion by the ministers. Sometimes either the Working Group or COREPER would reach complete agreement on an item, in which case it would go to the Council of Ministers as an 'A' point, that is an item which would be formally adopted without further discussion. As, in accordance with the Treaties, all meetings of the Council of Ministers had equal status, these 'A' points did not necessarily have to wait for the Labour and Social Affairs Council for adoption, though they usually did – the Minister in the Presidency concerned was usually keen to chalk up a 'success' and to have his name on the relevant legal instrument.

For three months of the year, including June, all meetings of the Council of Ministers were held in Luxembourg. So, in June 1978 I went to Luxembourg for my first meeting of the Council of Labour and Social Affairs. I don't remember much about that particular meeting, but the set-up was the same for all these meetings. Each Member State was allowed to have nine representatives for each item. Typically, these would be the Minister, Bill Nicholl, a Deputy Secretary from the Department of Employment (DE), the Assistant Secretary from DE responsible for EEC Coordination, Gerry Wilson, me, and the relevant experts from the Ministry. The Minister's Private Secretary usually tried to come, but we tried to discourage them, as it was 'our job' to look after the Ministers when they were in Brussels or Luxembourg.

Looking after Ministers, Parliamentarians and other senior officials was an important part of the job. The Foreign Office 'charged' the Department of Employment when they provided a car and driver for one of their Ministers. This was said to be quite expensive, when they were to be picked up at the airport late at night. I was therefore 'encouraged' to meet them myself. Accordingly, early in my stay, I went to the airport late one evening to meet the Chairman of the Manpower Services Commission at Brussels airport at Zaventem. He expressed his gratitude to me for turning out and I duly drove him to his hotel without incident.

A week or two later the PUSS, John Grant, arrived on the same plane. He was miffed that a proper driver hadn't been sent to meet him and was even more upset, when I took a wrong turning off the ring road and took a road that I did not know (the N2) into Brussels. A year or so before, John Rimington had upset John Grant, by insisting on driving him to Luxembourg for a Council Meeting. I don't recall what went wrong, but something did. Years later in the nineties, when he was no longer a Minister, John Grant came over for a meeting with the Labour and Social Affairs Commissioner, Henk Vredeling. John Morley had organised the meeting, but couldn't take Mr Grant back to the airport. He asked me to do so. I accepted with some trepidation, but, on this occasion, John Grant was very grateful. He nevertheless told me about the time John Rimington had taken him to Luxembourg. I was pleased to note that he did not talk about the time I had met him at the airport.

The last Minister that I drove anywhere was Lynda Chalker, who, at that time was PUSS in the Department of Health and Social Security. She, incidentally, was the most pleasant Minister that I ever had to deal with. She had come over for a meeting of the Council of Ministers and was staying overnight at Bill Nicholl's house. He asked me if I would pick her up on my way to the office, which I duly did. We were driving on the three lane one-way road round the Cinquantenaire, when a car cut in from the right and I had to swerve to avoid it, which I did.[15] Mrs Chalker congratulated me on my driving and no harm was done. I, however, reflected on what might have happened, if a Government Minister had been hurt, or worse, when I had been driving. I determined there and then never to drive a Minister again.

In the summer or early autumn of 1978, a House of Commons Committee decided to visit Brussels on a "fact-finding" mission. There were about ten of them, led by Renée Short. The leading Conservative was Nicholas Winterton. They were expecting a General Election to be called shortly and were all hyper-excited.[16] They were very rude in their dealings with Commission officials. Bill Nicholl invited the group to dinner one evening. He had a "robust debate" with Nicholas Winterton, who was one of the best debaters in the House of Commons. (Many years later, in the early nineties, Nicholas Winterton led a delegation from the House of Commons Committee on health. They were concerned about the Working Time Directive, which the=- Conservative

---

[15] The *Cinquantenaire* is a 30 hectare park to the east of the European quarter in Brussels. It was created in 1880 to mark the fiftieth anniversary of Belgian independence.
[16] Labour was expected to win that election, but, in the end, James Callaghan decided to wait until the following year. Early 1979 saw "the winter of discontent" and was followed by the election of the first Thatcher Government.

Government did not like at all. They were expected to be hostile. My boss in the Commission, Herman van Zonneveld, and I met them. On this occasion, they were very polite and, in any case, Herman was very good at dealing with hostile questioning.)

When I arrived in Brussels there was a Commission proposal on the table for a Directive providing for the progressive implementation of the principle of equal treatment for men and women in matters of social security. Although the proposal for a Directive did not apply to the fixing of the pension age, it posed considerable practical difficulties for the British and Irish Governments. In the Working Group and COREPER, we had stuck out for a seven-year implementation period, instead of the normal two years. About every other day before the Council meeting in December 1978, Otto Dibelius, who was then the Chairman of the Working Group, telephoned me to ask me if we had changed our position.

On the evening before the Council meeting, I arranged a meeting in the bar of the Charlemagne Hotel in Brussels between Stan Orme and Charles Haughey. Stan Orme was the Minister of State in the Department of Health and Social Security and a former Northern Ireland Minister. Charles Haughey was the Irish Minister for Social Security, an ardent Republican and a future Taoiseach. They knew each other and had previously been on opposite sides of the negotiating table. However, they had a brief, but amicable discussion and swore to stick out together for a seven-year transitional period. At the Council meeting the next day, the German Minister, Herr Ehrenberg, opened the discussion by saying that the main issue was the implementation period. In his view, a two-year was reasonable. What did other Ministers think? Mr Haughey? "That sounds reasonable to me!" he replied. Mr Orme? "That sounds reasonable to me!" was the same reply. As Gerry Wilson was fond of saying: "Collapse of stout party!"[17][18]

The following year, shortly before the General Election in May, the Secretary of State for Employment, Albert Booth, came to Brussels for a meeting. I asked him impertinently whether he expected to be Secretary of State after the election. He replied that it depended on three things: first he had to retain his marginal seat of Barrow-in-Furness; second, Labour had to win the election; and thirdly, Jim Callaghan had to reappoint him as Secretary of State. In the event, only the first of those three conditions was satisfied.

After the election, Jim Prior was appointed as Secretary of State for Employment. He came to the Council meeting in Luxembourg in June, accompanied by Lynda Chalker. Unusually, my wife, Jennifer, went to Luxembourg with me on this occasion. On the evening before the meeting, we all went for a meal in a pleasant village on the banks of the Moselle. Jennifer was rewarded for her presence by being chatted up by Jim Prior.

This was the first time I had met Lynda Chalker. She was there because the Department of Health and Social Security (DHSS) had taken an initiative to extend the Regulation dealing with, *inter alia*, reciprocal arrangements for health care – the E111 and later European Health Insurance Card (EHIC) – first to self-employed people and then to non-employed people. Lynda Chalker was quickly converted to the cause and became a strong and persistent advocate. This idea had been

---

[17] That story is true, but I have checked the wording of the Directive (79/7/EEC) and find that the implementation period was six years. I can only assume that Bill Nicoll worked his magic in COREPER and got the period changed to six years.

[18] This was one of Gerry Wilson's favourite expressions. It referred to the situation where one party took up a strong (and often unrealistic) negotiating position. Instead of trying to negotiate a compromise, the negotiators stuck to their position, but ended up collapsing and accepting the other party's proposition.

accepted by the Commission who had made a proposal. While many Member States were amenable to the idea, the proposal broke new ground in that, traditionally, Community labour law applied only to employees. I invited Maurice Ramond and Les Reffell from DHSS to our house in Overijse to discuss this and I think we persuaded Maurice of the logic of our arguments. We had the most difficulty with the Danes, who were obstinate in their opposition. Finally, they confided to me that they were not opposed to the health care arrangements – they said that similar bilateral arrangements were already in place – but they were worried that adoption of this Regulation would imply that the principle of free movement would be extended to everyone, whereas, at that time, it applied only to workers and their dependents. This, in turn, they feared, could give rise to large numbers of Germans settling in Denmark. In the end, a compromise was agreed, but I don't remember the precise wording.

Another aspect of my job was to cultivate a good relationship with officials in the European Commission, in my case mainly in Directorate-General V (DGV) – the Employment and Social Affairs Directorate-General. This, in itself, had two separate aspects. One was to get to know the people responsible for the work that directly affected the UK, in particular legislative proposals and matters relating to the European Social Fund, which was one of the few areas, where the UK was a net beneficiary from EEC funds. The second was to get to know the British officials, with the narrow objective that they might be helpful to us, and the wider objective of trying to assert a "British" dimension, into what was at that time a French dominated institution.

These issues were to some extent inter-related. Soon after the UK joined the EEC, a British national, Michael Shanks, had been appointed Director-General of DGV. A couple of years later, he was ousted from that post and replaced by Jean Degimbe, a Belgian, who had been *chef de cabinet* (head of the private office) of an influential French Commissioner. I never got to the bottom of that affair, in which UKREP was also alleged to be implicated. Suffice it to say, that some of the British nationals in the Commission had strong feelings on both sides of the argument. Many of the British officials wanted to have as little as possible to do with UKREP for a variety of reasons. Some felt let down by UKREP in the Shanks affair referred to above. Others felt that they had been let down by UKREP, when they had sought support in their bids for promotion. Others, particularly those who had come from the academic field had no affinity with UK national objectives, while yet others thought it prudent to distance themselves from the UK Government (Labour at that time) which was unenthusiastic about the European project. Two exceptions were John Morley, with whom I had worked in the Department of Employment, along with his colleague, David White, and Dr Bill Hunter, who worked in the Health and Safety Directorate in Luxembourg. I hasten to add that neither of them did anything improper, but we had a good working relationship.

Many Member States, including the UK, had "national experts" seconded to the Commission for a period of up to three years. One such expert, whose name I can't remember, came from the Northern Ireland Office to work in the European Social Fund. I had lunch with him just before he left and he boasted that he had made £100,000 for the UK during his time in Brussels. He had done this, legitimately, by ensuring that in internal discussions and rules, situations favourable to the UK were given due weight. It had not been the British Government's intention to replace him, but I argued that it would be foolish not to do so. While I was there, two young men were sent out from the Department of Employment as national experts, one after the other. It so happened that, first minor and then major reforms were carried out during these two periods. On my estimation, the first of these experts was able to increase, legitimately, the UK receipts by millions of pounds, while in the second case it was probably in the tens of million.

We were in Brussels at the height of the cold war. The IRA were also very active. The Foreign Office was very keen on security, not to say paranoid. The Representation occupied the seventh, eighth and ninth floors of an ordinary office block. The lift had been built to serve all floors, but the exits from the eighth and ninth floors had been blocked, so that everyone coming into the office had to report to the security desk on the seventh floor. One lunch time an "elderly" secretary came back from lunch and somehow managed to get stuck in the lift on the ninth floor. It was some time before someone on the ninth floor heard her frantic screams and arranged for someone to investigate.

I have already mentioned the assassination of the British Ambassador in The Hague. At about the same time a Belgian businessman was murdered near his home in Brussels. He lived in the same street as Christopher Tugendhat, one of the British EEC Commissioners. It was believed that Mr Tugendhat had been the intended target. After that an armed police guard was put outside the main door of the office block. One lunchtime, the policeman on duty undid the safety catch on his gun and sprayed gunshot round the square. Fortunately no-one was hurt, but the windows of the *Queen Victoria* pub were shattered.

All the First Secretaries had to do a turn as Duty Officer for a week. This involved going round the office late one evening and once at the weekend to make sure that all the safes were locked and no confidential papers were lying around. It was unusual to find anything, because everyone was conscious that security breaches were not looked on kindly. I went in one weekend, however, when a team of inspectors were over from London. They had been taken over a meeting room, used among other things for briefing journalists, as their office. I went in there and the table was littered with files marked "Confidential". I didn't say anything in my report, but went to speak to the Head of Chancery on the Monday morning.

The Duty Officer was also required to be available on call all the time to take emergency calls from London, or elsewhere. One Saturday evening, when I was on duty, we had been invited to a party given by one of the Security Officers. I was given a very frosty reception: *Where have you been all day? Security have been ringing you and you didn't answer your phone.* I replied that I had been at home all day. On the Monday morning I was summoned to appear before the Head of Chancery to account for my misdemeanours. Eventually, it transpired that my phone number had been copied wrongly on to the list at the security desk.

Quite often the phone would ring at home, but there was no-one on the line when you answered it. (Sounds familiar these days, but uncommon then!) On at least one occasion our son, Jon, who would have been eight or nine at the time, picked up the phone and shouted: *Bog off, you Russians!*

The Iron Curtain and the Berlin Wall

In the summer of 1980, we went as a family on holiday to Denmark, Norway and Sweden. We took the ferry back to Travemünde, in West Germany, which was right on the border with East Germany. We stopped to watch the Trabants driving out of East Germany. (Presumably these belonged to well-connected East Germans who could be "trusted" by the regime to go back after being tainted by western decadence.) I then decided to take a little side road and drive up to the iron curtain. It was real. A normal country road just came to a dead end, or, rather, petered out into dilapidation, before disappearing completely. On the right-hand side of the road was a farmhouse, a few metres from the massive barbed-wire fence which marked the border: it seemed likely that the iron curtain had cut through the farmer's land. At the side of the dilapidated road, a few metres short of the iron curtain was a big notice which said that this was the *Demokratische Deutsche Republik* (DDR), with words to the effect that anyone going beyond this point was liable to be shot. Beyond the iron curtain was a two-kilometre wide stretch of cleared barren land. In the middle of this stood a watch-tower, presumably situated there to shoot any East Germans who might try to escape.

In October of the previous year, Erik van Traa, the Dutch Counsellor for Social Affairs and doyen of the Social Questions Group, organised a visit of members of the group to Berlin, ostensibly to visit the European Centre for Vocational Education and Training, which was situated there. I don't remember anything about the training centre, but it was a memorable trip. At that time West Berlin was an enclave in East Germany – the DDR. Before we left I was advised that, if I wanted to visit East Berlin I would need to get permission from the British Governor's office in Berlin. I telephoned the office and asked if there was any reason why I shouldn't go to East Berlin. I can still hear the very snooty lady to whom I spoke replying: "There is *every* reason why you shouldn't go that weekend, as we are expecting a visit from Mr Brezhnev!"

Social Questions Group in Berlin, 5 October 1979
Otto Dibelius (Germany) left; Pascal Leonard (Ireland) centre left

We flew into West Berlin and my hotel was on the *Kurfürstendamm*, one of the liveliest streets in what was a very lively city. The hotel was not far from the *Kaiser-Wilhelm-Gedächtniskirche*, a ruined church that had been left as a reminder of the war. While we were there, we visited all the tourist sites in West Berlin and I was very impressed by the greenness of the city. The Brandenburg Gate and the old *Reichstag*, which stood on the borders of East and West Berlin were sorry sights. We also went to a Wagner opera, which I didn't enjoy very much.

As a holder of a British Diplomatic passport, I was expressly forbidden from going across the checkpoint into East Berlin. This was because the United Kingdom Government did not recognise the legitimacy of the incorporation of the Russian sector into the DDR. However, during the course of my stay, I **flew** in **over** East Germany. I stood on a hillock and **looked over** the Berlin Wall into East Berlin. The routes of the West Berlin *U-Bahn* (Underground railway system) had not been altered since the war; this meant that when I took the train from one part of West Berlin to another, I **travelled under** part of East Berlin; the train stopped eerily at two or three ghost stations in East Berlin; the doors didn't open and no-one got in or out. Finally, I went to Checkpoint Charlie and **looked through** the border into East Berlin.

View over Berlin Wall, including Hitler's Bunker

Some ten or eleven years later, when I was working for the European Commission, I went on a German language course, organised by the Goethe Institute. The enterprising young tutor arranged for a number of us to go to Berlin for a few days – a private trip at our own expense. We travelled by train overnight, changing at Cologne. The journey from Cologne through what was by then the ex-DDR seemed endless. (Curiously, I don't remember anything about the return journey.) Many changes had occurred in the years between my two visits, though much remained the same.

On the first day we had a meeting with a civic official. He predicted that it would take 25 years to unify the city. At the time, it seemed an awfully long time, but now, over 25 years later, from what I understand it was probably about right. We visited the sights that I had visited before. But we also went to new ones. I don't normally rave over museums, but the Pergamon Museum in what had until recently been East Berlin was overwhelming.[19] We also went to Potsdam to the Sanssouci Palace.[20] This was very beautiful. I went back to Checkpoint Charlie and visited a museum there. It was only then that I realised that over 20 million citizens of the USSR had been killed in the Second World War. I also went on a ride in a canal boat around the old Berlin Wall, parts of which were still standing at that time.

King of the Castle: July to December 1981

On 1st July 1981, it was the UK's turn to have the Presidency of the Council of Ministers. This meant that British ministers and officials chaired all the meetings of the Council, COREPER and Council working groups. In my case this meant that I was to chair the Social Questions Working Group for the next six months. This was a great privilege, but also a daunting prospect. However, since I had passed the Administrative Class competition in 1971, I thought I was good at chairing meetings. At least I could provide a contrast in style to my predecessor, Erik van Traa, who was shrewd and had a strong personality, but was rather lazy. I believed that the secret of chairmanship lay in good preparation and a clear understanding of what was achievable. Accordingly, before each meeting of the Working Group, usually on the Monday,

---

[19] The Pergamon Museum was constructed over a period of twenty years, from 1910 to 1930. It houses monumental buildings such as the Pergamon Altar, the Ishtar Gate of Babylon, the Market Gate of Miletus reconstructed from the ruins found in the Middle East, as well as the Mshatta Facade.

[20] *Sanssouci* is the summer palace of Frederick the Great, King of Prussia, in Potsdam, near Berlin. It was built between 1745 and 1747.

I called a meeting with Enzo Chioccioli and his subordinate responsible for the dossiers under discussion and the responsible Commission officials. We went through the report of the previous meeting and examined the positions of those delegations who had reservations on the various points that we wanted to discuss. We then discussed what possible modifications could be made to the text to accommodate their concerns, without losing the support of those who took a different position.

A new Commission had taken office in January 1981. Gaston Thorn had replaced Roy Jenkins as President. Ivor Richard, QC, a Welsh barrister and Labour party nominee, had replaced Henk Vredeling as Commissioner for Employment and Social Affairs. Mr Vredeling had been Commissioner for many years and so most of the proposals for legislation he had put forward had been either adopted or put on the backburner. By July, Ivor Richard had not had time to put forward any proposals of his own. Consequently, the menu that was at my disposal consisted of a complicated amendment to the Regulation (1408/71) dealing with social security coordination; a Directive on the protection of workers against exposure to lead at work; and a similar Directive about exposure to asbestos. Erik van Traa had not managed to get agreement on the social security amendment and, as far as I can remember, neither did I.

The asbestos proposal had not been discussed in the Working Group before. I arranged a number of meetings on it and reasonable progress was made. But it was unlikely that there would be time to reach agreement during the British Presidency. This may appear dilatory, but the timing was as follows. Although, it was a six-month Presidency, in reality, less than four months were available for discussion in the Working Group. Everything closed down for four weeks in

August (I was heavily criticised by van Traa and others for arranging a meeting early in September!) and the Council meeting was held in early December, with COREPER before that. It was the practice to allow at least three weeks between each meeting on the same dossier: this just about gave enough time for the Council Secretariat to prepare their report, have it translated into the other five languages and circulate it to the capitals, where officials could consider the report, react to any compromises that had been proposed and decide whether they wished to change their negotiating positions.

So, the main item on my agenda was the lead directive. The debate centred on the amount of lead that workers could have in their blood and still be safe. The figures discussed ranged from 45 micrograms to 60. (I don't remember now what the other factor was.) The Italians, who were led by a very nice man from a research institute, wanted the figure to be set at 45, in order to put pressure on the Italian Government. At the other end of the scale, not for the first time, were the Brits. Their situation was complicated because they had just produced domestic legislation, which had been agreed after a long period of domestic consultation and negotiation.

As was usually the case, I managed to reduce the areas of disagreement to half a dozen key points. I produced a draft compromise, which I managed to "sell" to Gerry Wilson and Enzo Chioccioli. The timing was crucial: if it was made available too soon, the delegations would have time to unpick it; if it was too late, they would simply say that they needed time to study it. In the event, I think we probably got the timing about right and the proposal was on the agenda of the Council of Ministers, chaired by Norman Tebbit. The plan was that there would be a brief Council meeting and then I would be sent off to chair an extraordinary meeting of the Working

Group. At that meeting, after a long unproductive discussion, I came up with a new compromise – an adrenalin rush. This new compromise was agreed by all members of the Working Group and we broke for lunch thinking we had agreement.

During the lunch break, however, the Germans let it be known that they could not agree. When the Council Meeting resumed, I was again sent off to chair another meeting of the Working Group. This meeting had not been planned and we spent some time finding an available room and then interpreters. We eventually had some desultory discussions, before we heard that it was snowing in London; Mr Tebbit needed to get back and the Council meeting had already finished. Before that, Mr Tebbit had worked hard to get agreement, but the Germans were adamant and it would not have made any difference if we had stayed all night.

At COREPER the following week, we put forward a further compromise, but no agreement was reached. However, the wording of the Directive (82/605/EEC) adopted the following year under the Belgian Presidency was almost identical to that we had proposed in COREPER.

Towards the end of November, I had got very frustrated by the lack of result for my hard work. I decided to take up painting. Jennifer bought me some painting material for Christmas and I painted my first picture, with some help from my mother, in Skegness shortly afterwards. (My son, Jon, still has this picture, which is one of the best I ever did!)

I did have some small successes during my period as Chairman of the Working Group. I was very pleased to get adopted a Regulation implementing the extension of social security arrangements to self-employed workers. This was a very long and complicated Regulation, which was necessary to apply the agreement some years earlier. It had been drawn up following lengthy discussions in a Commission Working Group (called the Administrative Commission). Only about three people in the world understood it and I was not one of them. It was very important for the Department of Health and Social Security (DHSS). With some pressure from me and more from DHSS, the Commission made a proposal in November. I called a meeting of the Working Group immediately and it was agreed within twenty minutes – about 5 pages a minute! It went to Council as an 'A' point.

I also arranged with Hywel Jones, who at that time was a Director in the Training Division of DGV, for a draft resolution on the employment of disabled people to be drawn up. This was adopted at the Council meeting in December.

Norman Tebbit stories

The original inspiration for this book was to collect together a number of stories involving Norman Tebbit. I had first met Mr Tebbit, when I went to be interviewed for the job as Private Secretary to Robin Chichester-Clark in 1972. At that time the young Mr Tebbit was Parliamentary Private Secretary (PPS) to Mr Chichester-Clark. A PPS is an unpaid position, which is the first rung on the ladder towards becoming a Government minister. I did not get that job.

The next time I saw him was in September 1981. He had just been appointed as Secretary of State for Employment in succession to James Prior. Every six months, there was a meeting in Brussels of a body called the Standing Committee on Employment (SEC). This was chaired by the President of the Council of Ministers (in this case Norman Tebbit). Ministers from all Member States, the Commissioner and representatives of employers' and trades union organisations were present. Its basic political purpose was to give the trades union an opportunity to air their grievances in front of the Commission and ministers.

Traditionally, the President read out his "Conclusions" from the meeting at the end. I was invited to a meeting in Caxton House, the new Headquarters of the Department of Employment, to prepare the Secretary of State for the meeting. The full panoply of DE officials were there from Donald Derx (Deputy Secretary) downwards. They were reassuring Mr Tebbit that it was a routine meeting, which would not raise any problems. I felt it incumbent on me to say that I did not see it that way: many of the trade union representatives were from French-speaking unions, who, unlike the TUC at that time, were pro-European and would be seeking to exert pressure for more European Community action on workers' rights. Mr Tebbit replied: "I shall just remind them, who won the battle of Waterloo!"

It was customary for the President's Conclusions to be negotiated during a break before the end of the meeting. On this occasion the main participants were Enzo Chioccioli, John Morley from the Commission, Bill Callaghan from the TUC and myself. I do not recall the contents, but, if John Morley was involved, I am sure they were sensible.[21] There was an almighty row! The trades union representatives complained bitterly and the meeting ended in uproar. At least I had the satisfaction of having warned Mr Tebbit that it wouldn't be a stroll in the park. It transpired afterwards that the real reason why some of the trade union representatives were upset was

---

[21] Sir William Callaghan received a knighthood in 2007 for distinguished service to health and safety.

that the Conclusions had been drafted in English and they could not understand them!

After the UK Presidency, Mr Tebbit was a regular attender at meetings of the Council of Ministers. He was a trained pilot and wanted to fly himself to one or more of the meetings, much to the chagrin of Donald Derx. I remember him coming by private plane on at least one occasion, but I don't think he actually piloted it himself.

On one occasion, he was staying with Bill Nicholl. We were invited to a dinner at Bill and Helen's house. There was a friendly, half-joking debate between Mr Tebbit and Bill about the role of the party in government. Mr Tebbit argued that during their first term in government, the ministers were like the ship's captain – the guardian of the ship. But, if they were elected for a second term, they became the ship's masters.

Bill, himself, had a fund of colourful stories. His home Department was the Board of Trade. Some years before, he had been sent to India to work. Bill was a very accomplished linguist and decided he wanted to learn the local language. He found an old man who was willing to give him lessons. As was to be expected, Bill learned very quickly and was not shy at showing off his prowess with the locals. To his chagrin, every time he did so, people started laughing. In the end, he couldn't contain himself and asked: "Why, when I speak your language, does everyone burst out laughing?" The reply came: "You speak the language very well, you have a good vocabulary and a good knowledge of grammar, but you sound like an old man with no teeth!"

In late 1981 or early 1982, the Commission, at the behest of Ivor Richard, produced a proposal for a Directive on part time work and another on temporary work. These came up for an orientation debate in the Council of Ministers. Norman Tebbit had read the Explanatory Memorandum of the temporary work proposal and noted that it included a statement that temporary workers should enjoy the same benefits in kind as permanent workers. It gave the right to equal access to a company swimming pool as an example. Mr Tebbit ridiculed this. Ivor Richard, who was a big man, replied that if he had a swimming pool, he would willingly invite the Secretary of State to join him in it. To which Mr Tebbit retorted: "If you were in it, there wouldn't be room for anyone else!" All this greatly amused and puzzled the representatives of the other Member States: Council meetings were supposed to be serious and polite, i.e. dull and boring!

There was a tradition that each Presidency invited Ministers of Labour from all the other Member States to an informal meeting in their country. Attendance was restricted to one Minister and two officials per Member State. In the case of the UK, Donald Derx used to go from London and Gerry Wilson from UKREP. This was about the only occasion when Gerry Wilson "pulled rank". When it came to the UK Presidency, we had a much bigger delegation. So the first informal meeting I went to was held in the Intercontinental Hotel in London in 1981. I do not remember much about the meeting itself, but I do remember a splendid meal – with English wine – in the magnificent setting of Lancaster House. I did not go to the Belgian informal meeting, but the Danish Social Affairs Counsellor, who had replaced Morten Fenger during my Presidency – gave me a personal invitation to the meeting in Copenhagen in the autumn of 1982.

In the spring of 1983, I was again invited to the German informal meeting in Bonn. It was just before the General Election in the UK. Norman Tebbit came to that meeting. He seemed to be enjoying the relief from domestic politics. Alan

Hatfull, the British Labour attaché in Bonn, had persuaded Mr Tebbit that he would like to visit a German Vocational Training Centre after the informal meeting had finished. His return plane had been booked to accommodate that. However, the day before, Mr Tebbit decided that he would prefer to work in the hotel room in the afternoon rather than visit the training centre. I was asked to see if that could be arranged, as the room had been booked only until midday. The following morning, there was a discussion about the proposal for a Directive on part-time work, where, not for the first time, the UK was in a minority of one in opposing it. Mr Tebbit was having a difficult time. In the course of the discussion, I received a message from the Germans to say that Mr Tebbit could keep the room. I was sitting next to him. I wrote a message: *Secretary of State, you can stay in your room all day, if you want.* On reflection, not very elegant. The reply came back very quickly: *I shall probably wish that I had!*

At the end of the same meeting, the Greek Minister, as was the tradition, in a long speech, thanked the German Minister for his hospitality and invited his fellow ministers to an informal meeting in Greece in the autumn. He noted that the previous evening we had visited a cathedral where the one Christian God was worshipped and it was very splendid, but, he added: *In Greece we have many temples and many gods ...* Mr Tebbit said in an aside to us: *Another example of Greek overmanning!* Unfortunately, like the rest of us, he was listening to the interpreter through his headset, which meant that his aside could be heard by everyone in the room.

I saw a different side to Mr Tebbit the last time I met him. We went to Luxembourg for the Council of Ministers meeting in June 1983. We were all assembled in the UK's room in the Council building with HM Ambassador to Luxembourg. Mr

Tebbit was late arriving. When he did arrive I came to understand the expression: *he had a face like thunder!* I don't know whether he had come on a commercial flight or in a private plane. Either way, he had not had a smooth passage through the Luxembourg border controls and he was very angry.

Life outside the office

We lived in Brussels for five and half years between February 1978 and September 1983. The start was inauspicious, especially for Jennifer.

My predecessor, Tim Biddescombe, had booked us in to the Hotel Derby, where we had dark and dingy back rooms, in which we slept for the first eight nights. We had got the boys, who were 7 and 10, into the British School of Brussels, which was in Tervuren about 15 km from the centre of Brussels. Jennifer's first experience of driving on the right was to drive from the hotel in an almost new car to the school. The first thing she had to do was to negotiate the complicated Montgomery roundabout, which was a test for any driver – I always avoided it, whenever possible. She did it without mishap!

We had hoped to take over Tim Biddescombe's house, which was in Woluwe St Pierre within the city boundaries and well situated for shops, the school and the office. However, as in Swaziland, there was a shortage of accommodation and that house was allocated to Charles Drake-Francis, a career diplomat, and his family.

The following Sunday, however, we moved into a very large four bedroomed house in Kasteelstraat, about 14 kilometres from the centre of Brussels, in the parish of Overijse. Brussels is a bilingual, predominantly French, 'island' in Flanders, which is Dutch-speaking.[22] There is a strip of land, no more than 20 kilometres wide — and less in parts, to the south and east of Brussels, which is Dutch-speaking. South of that comes Wallonia, which is French speaking.

Kasteelstraat 34 (2021)

The town council in Overijse was militant in its defence of the Dutch language. All official documents were in Dutch, including notes from the Post Office. For that reason I

---

[22] Flemish is a dialect of Dutch. After the war, a linguistic Commission was set up, with the consequence that a common Dutch language is taught in Belgian and Dutch schools and used in official documents in both countries.

decided fairly early on that I ought to try to learn Dutch, because, when the postman put a card in the letterbox, it was difficult to work out whether we had to collect a parcel, or pay a fine or something else.

An extreme example of linguistic intolerance occurred to Wendy Allman. They lived not far from us. Their sons, Steve and Max, were a few years older than our boys and also went to the British School. They were good athletes and were chosen to represent Belgium for their age group at an international athletics meeting in France. They needed a document from the Town Hall in Overijse. Wendy was a French teacher. She spoke very good French and passable German. But she didn't speak Dutch. She went along to the Town Hall with her request in French, English and German, but the officials pretended not to understand her. The boys didn't get their documents.

On the other hand, Peter lost his Belgian Identity Card. Possibly with Wendy's experience in mind, I went to the local Police Station, armed with a well-rehearsed request in Dutch. The policeman was impressed and we went on to have an interesting conversation in French and English – and Peter got a new Identity Card!

Similarly, some ten years later, Dieter Kaschke drove over to Brussels from Bonn. He took us in his car to the *Zonienwoud* (*Forêt de Soignes*). We parked the car somewhere near the border of Overijse and Tervuren and went for a walk. When we got back, someone had bashed the car and Dieter wanted to report it to the police. We went to the police station in Overijse and again I had prepared something in my head to say in Dutch. Again the policeman was most helpful and produced relevant documentation for Dieter to sign in any of four languages. That would not have happened if I had gone in speaking French.

Generally speaking at that time most Flemish people were good linguists. As a diplomat, I was entitled to duty-free petrol (but only from Shell garages). There was a convenient Shell garage not far from our house on the *Steenweg op Brussel*. One evening, on my way home from work, I called in at the Shell garage to fill up with petrol. There was an old lady at the cash desk. She was speaking German to the customer in front of me. She saw my petrol vouchers and spoke to me in English. She was a native Dutch speaker and almost certainly spoke French.

Jezuz-Eik church, Overijse

On the other hand, native French speakers sometimes had problems. Our neighbours in *Kasteelstraat* were French speaking, though José was bilingual. Their son, Jerry, who was a teenager, when we arrived, spoke French and had a big problem learning Dutch. The consequence was that he had great difficulty in getting a job, because nearly all jobs in the area required employees to be bilingual. He is a brilliant artist and now owns an art gallery in Ixelles.

Kasteelstraat was part of a large post-war development two kilometres from the centre of Overijse, which is a picturesque old Flemish town. The area is famous for growing large (and expensive) dessert grapes. A few hundred metres from our house was a small shopping centre with a very large Delhaize supermarket. In the vicinity there were several other shops, including a newsagent, a fine delicatessen, a pharmacy, a shop selling mainly sports clothing and a cycle shop. The newsagent sold English newspapers. When I came back to Skegness to see my parents, my father used to have to order a copy of the *Observer* if I wanted one. At the shop in Belgium there was a pile of *Observers* a metre high from about 11:00 am on Sundays and a similar pile of *Sunday Times*.

In order to go from our house into Brussels (or anywhere else apart from to the south) one had to cross the *Forêt de Soignes*.

Forêt de Soignes

This is a vast (4421 hectare)[23] forest at the south-eastern edge of Brussels, consisting of mainly beech and oak trees. It is criss-crossed with main roads, minor roads, cycle paths, footpaths and other tracks. It is a wonderful place to go to fill one's lungs with fresh air.

Brussels, itself, is a marvellous place to live in or near. Bill Bryson, in his book *Neither here nor there: Travels in Europe*, wrote that he came to Brussels, saw the *Grand'Place*, decided there was nothing else to see and caught the next train to Luxembourg. I can understand that to a certain extent. The *Grand'Place* is exceptional. I went there hundreds of times, but never failed to marvel at its majestic splendour. But away from the *Grand'Place*, the many other jewels are often hidden away from the casual visitor.

The *Grand'Place* in Brussels

---

[23] 2017 estimate.

For much of Brussels was destroyed, not by the bombs, but by the bulldozers that transformed the city in the nineteen fifties and sixties. But the jewels are there to be found: the churches, palaces, squares, parks, museums and small houses, such as those belonging to Erasmus or Victor Horta.

From where we lived, we needed a car to go anywhere beyond walking distance. (There was a bus service into Brussels which went along the *Steenweg op Brussel*, but we never learned how to use it.) We could drive into the centre of Brussels, but normally we drove to a large shopping centre at Demey and took the metro from there. Within forty minutes of leaving home, we could be in the centre of a capital city with all its shops, restaurants, cinemas and other attractions. There were about a dozen cinemas in the centre of Brussels. There was also a cinema complex at the end of the metro line at Heysel, with over twenty screens and a number of restaurants and boutiques. At any one time there would be a dozen or so films that could be watched in the original English language.

Bruges: our favourite destination for a day trip

Back to "The Smoke" 2

I managed to extend my stay in Brussels to five and a half years, a record stay in UKREP at the time. (The record was beaten by Keith Masson, who succeeded my successor, Bob Niven.) In the August before we were due to return, we came back on leave to our house in Bushey, which had not been well looked after. We had already decided that we wanted to look for a bigger house and decided on a house in Watford.

We left Brussels on the first Saturday in September. Our belongings had been put on a removal van and were due to be delivered on the Monday. We travelled in two cars with two teenage boys. We were booked on a hovercraft from Calais to Ramsgate, but the seas were exceptionally rough and nothing was leaving Calais. (One ship had left early in the morning, but had been unable to get into Dover harbour and had returned to Calais some twelve hours later – Jennifer's worst nightmare.) Calais was gridlocked. Eventually, we drove in convoy and found a hotel a short distance from the sea at Cap Blanc-Nez. This was a *Logis de France*. At that time the accommodation in two-star hotels was very primitive, but the food in the *Logis de France* was always excellent.

We stayed there until Monday, when we finally got a hovercraft over to England. When we got to customs, we had to import two cars, which we had bought duty free and about 35 opened bottles of spirits and liqueurs, which we had also bought duty-free. Importing the cars was relatively straightforward, as there was no duty to pay. Duty was payable on the booze. The Customs Officer was very friendly, but spent ages assessing the contents of each bottle and the duty payable. It was dark when we left Ramsgate in convoy. The M25 was not yet open, so we had to find our way from the Dartford Tunnel to Bushey via North London. This took several hours, not least, because I took a wrong turning at one point. When we got back we discovered that an enormous removal van had been driven round our estate several times before we arrived.

I was entitled to ten weeks' leave, which I insisted on taking. I was determined to take it anyway, but I did not realise until I received my first pay statement, that I was still on the FCO's books and therefore entitled to a resettlement payment – so I was actually paid more for not working than when I went back to work!

By this time (1983) there was much more scope for negotiation about postings than there had been twenty years earlier. I was offered a job in the Industrial Relations Division of the Department of Employment. My section was called IRA3. It was a proper policy job. We had policy responsibility for many of the individual rights under the Industrial Relations Act 1971. This included, in particular, unfair dismissals. We also had policy responsibility for the Employment Appeals Tribunal (EAT) and the Industrial Tribunals in both England and Wales and Scotland. My boss, Douglas Tallintyre, was also line manager of the Secretaries of the Industrial Tribunals in London and Glasgow. I had one SEO (Geoff Bobker) three HEOs, an EO (Executive Officer), a Clerical Officer and a Clerical Assistant.

I arrived at the entrance to Caxton House on 17 October 1983 and travelled in the lift with Tom King, who was also taking up his new post as Secretary of State for Employment on the same day – he was taking over from Norman Tebbit.

I worked there for three years. During that time I had regular contact with ministers. Tom King was Secretary of State, followed by Lord (David) Young, with Kenneth Clarke as Paymaster-General, also in the Cabinet. Other ministers included the Hon. Peter Morrison, John Selwyn Gummer,

David Trippier, who was small firms minister and Peter Bottomley, who was a very nice man and with whom I had the most contact.

My friend, Brian Smith, had worked with Ken Clarke, when he had been in the Ministry of Health, and always spoke very highly of him. I only recall one meeting with him and I also was suitably impressed. The Prime Minister, Margaret Thatcher, was always looking for ways to reduce the burdens on business. By the time of this meeting in 1986, she had already had six years of purges, which, in our case, meant trying to reduce workers' rights. One day, Jim Galbraith, my Under-Secretary, called a meeting to say that the Prime Minister had called for a further review of all employment legislation with a view to getting rid of anything that could be abolished. The civil servants responsible were required to produce a single sheet of paper in respect of each right, saying why it had been introduced and justifying (or not) its continuing existence. These sheets were to go in Ken Clarke's Red (ministerial) Box that evening and to be discussed with him the following morning. A large number of sheets were produced. Ken Clarke is (or was) a barrister. Somewhere in this mass of paper, there was a small mistake or weak argument. (I don't think it was on one of my sheets!) Ken Clarke seized on this and sought an explanation.

Under the Industrial Relations Act the Secretary of State was required to review each year the upper limits on the amount of compensation the industrial tribunals were allowed to award, for example, in respect of unfair dismissal. I carried out this review. It involved writing to the CBI and TUC and then submitting a report to ministers (normally Peter Bottomley) with a recommendation. I usually put the limit as high as I could and I think each year my recommendations were accepted. I had to learn a new bit of parliamentary procedure. Orders had to be drafted (by the DE Solicitor) and adopted by a Resolution of both Houses of Parliament.

There was never a debate in the House of Commons, but always one in the House of Lords. This was tricky. DE did not usually have a Minister in the House of Lords. Two of the most prominent industrial relations lawyers in the country – Lord McCarthy and Lord Wedderburn were members of the House of Lords. Although this was a very minor piece of legislation, it was technically quite complex. The first year I was there the Government found an obscure Lord to take the Orders through the House of Lords. Fortunately, I don't remember his name. He was very nervous and I told him at least three times what he had to say, but when the time came he completely fluffed his lines. On most occasions the Lords are very gentle with their colleagues (or were then) and this was no exception, so the Orders went through without further ado. The last time I did this review, Lord Strathclyde was the Minister responsible. He was very young, but was already a Minister in the Board of Trade (or whatever it was called at the time!) He was very able and took the issues on board without any problems.

My responsibilities in relation to the EAT and industrial tribunals introduced me for the first and last time to the English and Scottish judicial systems. I had regular contact with the Lord Chancellor's Department. There were two big and perennial policy issues. The judiciary was independent of the Executive and fiercely defended its independence. Nevertheless the taxpayer paid their salaries, which were not insignificant and the Permanent Secretary of DE had to account to Parliament for his expenditure. The industrial tribunals had been inefficient and it was our job to try to make them more efficient. This was not an easy task, but one that we had to keep plugging away at.

The other big issue was summarised in the word *legalism*. The tribunals had originally been set up with the aim of providing a relatively cheap and informal mechanism for settling disputes (usually in relation to dismissal) between individuals and their (former) employers. But, as time went on, a considerable body of case law had built up. As losing a case of unfair dismissal was detrimental to the balance sheet and reputation of employers, many companies briefed barristers to argue their case. This in turn meant that workers and trade unions also needed to brief barristers to argue their case. The 'simple' procedure had become expensive and long-winded. I remember writing many policy papers on *legalism*, but I'm not sure that we made much progress.

One area where we did have some success was in the development of the role of individual conciliation officers within the Advisory, Conciliation and Arbitration Service (ACAS). Their role was to try to reach an agreement between the parties, before the complaint was heard by an industrial tribunal. Where this could be achieved it was beneficial to the employer (time and legal costs) to the worker (quicker settlement) and the taxpayer. (Conciliation Officers were much cheaper than tribunals.)

The DE had no power in relation to the enforcement or interpretation of the legislation. This did not prevent people writing to their MP or the Secretary of State. On the contrary, we received hundreds of letters each year, mostly from members of the public who considered they had been maltreated in some way. When members of the public wrote to their MP, the normal practice was for the MP to forward the letter to the Secretary of State for his comments. Such letters were put in an orange folder – an 'orange jacket' – and sent to the relevant Head of Section (in these cases me) to draft a reply.

The orange jackets had a strict deadline of about ten days. I usually gave them to one of my HEOs, usually Ian Drummond, to draft the reply. This went back to the Minister (usually a junior minister) under my responsibility. Ian Drummond was one of the most competent officials at that level that I ever came across. In one of his annual reports I described him as the 'Ian Botham' of the Department.[24] Ian Drummond had an almost encyclopaedic knowledge of the Industrial Relations Act and the ensuing case law. He was hard-working and good at drafting letters. Even he struggled to keep up with the flow of correspondence, for the orange jackets were only the tip of the iceberg. Most members of the public wrote directly to the Secretary of State. These letters were sent directly to the HEO responsible (in our case Ian Drummond) for him to reply on behalf of the minister. I rarely saw these, but it was a constant cause for concern, that there was always a backlog of unanswered letters.

---

[24] Ian Botham (later Sir Ian Botham) was an England cricketer with a strong personality and immense all-round talent as bowler, batsman and fielder, who was in his prime in the early eighties.

Something different: The Technical and Vocational Education Initiative (TVEI)

The Industrial Relations job was a 'proper' job, which I enjoyed and which I think I performed competently. Nevertheless it was the tradition in the Department that one did a job for about three years and then moved on. I still had ambitions for promotion and I thought I ought to get some management experience. (I had had practically no management responsibilities for 17 years and none at a more senior level.) Following discussions with Personnel, Ruth Le Guen got in touch with me. Ruth had been coming out to Brussels in relation to a Commission proposal on equal opportunities for men and women. (The lead spokesperson for the Commission on this proposal, incidentally, was Odile Quintin, who was to become my Director later on – see later chapter.) Ruth had been promoted to Assistant Secretary and was now the number two in the TVEI Unit in the Training Agency of the Manpower Services Commission.

The Technical and Vocational Education Initiative was a programme that had been set up to introduce an understanding of the world of work into the curriculum of secondary schools. It was an ambitious (and expensive) project. Hitherto, it had been run as a pilot from offices in Grays Inn Road in London, but it was now being extended to all Local Education Authorities who wished to participate. A dozen or so Advisers had been appointed throughout Great Britain to 'sell' the initiative to local authorities, to advise schools and to monitor progress. These Advisers were mostly people who had already been secondary head teachers. I was 48 at the time and most of the advisers were about my age. They were paid as Senior Principals, which was one grade higher than me. They were all dedicated, enthusiastic and articulate.

These existing advisers, though reporting to Ruth in London, were based around the country. It had been decided that more advisers would be appointed later in the year (September 1987) and that they would be based in eight English regional centres (normally in or near the Training Agency Regional Office) and in Cardiff and Glasgow (not Edinburgh!). It had also been decided that Regional Team Managers (SEOs) should be appointed to run these offices (control of budgets, etc.) and the number of Project Manager posts (HEO) providing the support to the Advisers should also be increased and based in the regional teams. What Ruth wanted was someone to manage these regional teams. (I use the word 'regional' as shorthand – Scotland and Wales are of course not regions!) I took the job.

My first job was to appoint the Regional Team Managers (RTM). The posts had already been advertised and a large number of applications received. Michael Jennings, who had been doing the job for the whole of the UK had already been appointed as RTM for the South East and was moving to Basingstoke. Willie Robertson had been the Project Manager in Glasgow and he was expected to be a shoo-in as Scottish Team Manager. I insisted on interviewing him first, but did appoint him. There was, however, a man doing a similar job in Wales. After interviewing him, I decided to look at the other candidates and eventually appointed someone else. I took the applications for the other posts home and drew up a short list for each one. Having just come from Industrial Relations, I ignored all the rules of best practice and interviewed nearly all the candidates on my own! Apart from the RTM for London, which took a fair time to sort out, all the RTMs took up post fairly quickly.

We also had to appoint Project Managers (HEOs) in each location, usually about two in each location. I left Michael Jennings to organise this in cooperation with the new RTMs. Nearly all the existing Project Managers based in Grays Inn Road decided to leave, so that, within the space of a few months we had an almost completely new administrative team. In addition to the regional teams, I had to set up a support office in Head Office in Grays Inn Road. This took some time, but eventually I appointed an SEO (George Anderson), two HEOs (Simon Attwood and Peter Drummond), an EO and one or two clerical workers. So in the end I had about 100 staff in 11 different locations and an administrative budget of well over £1 million. (The Programme Budget - the money given to schools - was over £100 million, but I was not accountable for that.)

In my previous job, a project was established to set up a paperless office! (I don't think it ever materialised.) When I moved to TVEI, I thought it should be possible to set up an electronic system of communication between my ten offices. (We could have called it *email*, but that would have been too fanciful!) I discovered that the Training Agency was working on such a system. I was told that I would have to buy in to their system. The problem was that they had already been working on it for two years and it had run into all sorts of technical difficulties. We discussed the communication issue at one of our early RTMs meetings. Ian Popham, the East Midlands RTM, said there was a new device called a Fax machine, which we could purchase for about £20. So, we introduced the Fax to the Training Agency.

The relationship between the career civil servants and the Advisers was potentially a difficult one. We, the civil servants, were responsible for ensuring that the money was well spent, but we were all, apart from Ruth, junior to them. On the whole, I had good relations with the advisers. Some of the regional teams worked well, others less well! I decided from the beginning to have a meeting of Regional Team Managers every month, usually in Grays Inn Road. With hindsight these must have been quite expensive, but I do think we created a good team spirit and that these meetings contributed to the coherence and success of the operation.

One of the attractions of the job for me was that it involved a lot of travelling. Although I had travelled widely in Europe and in Africa, I had done relatively little travelling in the UK. First of all, I had to manage the 9 teams that were based outside London. I visited each of these offices at least once a year.

Secondly, each Local Education Authority taking part in the scheme had an 'Annual Review'. These reviews were chaired usually by someone from Head Office and were designed to monitor how the money had been spent and to make suggestions for improvements. I was supposed to chair some of these meetings. I did this, but I never liked doing it, because I never felt confident about the educational aspects of the review. These reviews, of course, took place in the Local Education Authority area that was being reviewed.

Thirdly, the 'Powers That Be' in TVEI were great believers in conferences and I attended several during my period in TVEI. The first one was held in Bawtry in Yorkshire. It was a very intense conference. Part of TVEI was about the management of change in education, but at that time the 'regionalisation' and expansion of the programme created a good deal of tension within the organisation. This boiled over at this conference and I remember driving back from Bawtry wondering whether I had done right to join this strange organisation! The next of these conferences was in Derby in

September 1987. It was the first time all the new and old advisers had got together. On the whole, I think that Conference went rather better than the previous one (which wasn't difficult!).

At dinner one evening, we were discussing the location of the conference. One of the new advisers (Keith Greenwood) joked that it would have been better and cheaper to hold the conference in Majorca. I replied: "It probably would, but who is going to answer the PQ?" This amused the advisers and every time I met Keith Greenwood afterwards he said "Who is going to answer the PQ?" The background to this exchange was that, as a Whitehall civil servant my immediate reaction to anything out of the ordinary was that it would provoke a Parliamentary Question (PQ) from some MP or other and some civil servant would have to draft a reply. To an outsider the abbreviation 'PQ' was completely unknown and my reaction a source of great amusement. Throughout my career and afterwards I have tried to avoid acronyms and abbreviations. This was not true of all my colleagues. I have to say that the worst offenders were in the fields of education and training, where much of what was written was incomprehensible to the uninitiated (and me!).

So, during these three years, I went to all the places where we had out-stationed offices: Basingstoke, Bristol, Cardiff, Birmingham, Nottingham, Leeds, Manchester, Newcastle and Glasgow. In addition I also went to Warrington, Inveraray, Melrose and Hawick in the Borders and Edinburgh, as well as Bawtry, Derby, somewhere else in Derbyshire, Sunningdale and Carmarthen. The two visits to Inveraray were particularly memorable. Our host in the Borders was a retired Scottish Rugby Union international. The hotel we stayed in had *lottie* on the menu, which was the dialect word for 'monkfish' (*lotte* in French).

Judith Black, one of the most senior advisers (in terms of

length of service, not age!) also managed to arrange two visits to France – to Caen and Lille – to see how the French arranged things. On the back of these visits I applied successfully for a Western European Union bursary to spend a lengthy period of time in France studying arrangements in France for the transition from school to working life. However, the process for awarding the bursary was protracted and, by the time I was told I had been successful, I had moved on to my next job and I couldn't spare the time to do it.

Eastern Europe

Towards the end of 1989, my role at TVEI was changing and my post was being transferred to Sheffield. I did not want to go to Sheffield, mainly because I preferred, in the longer term, to work in a DE Headquarters policy environment, rather than in the executive agencies of the Manpower Services Commission. I had just turned 50 and I decided that I was no longer going to go for jobs that would improve my promotion prospects, but to go for jobs that would interest me, particularly in the area of international relations.

There was, in fact, only one job in the Department at my level that fell into that category, and which was likely to be available. This was the post which dealt with relations with the International Labour Organisation (ILO). It was a fairly low-profile post, but involved taking a lead role in the negotiations that took place each year in Geneva on the formulation of ILO Conventions. I also knew that the current occupant of the post was looking for a move. My friend, Bob David, with whom I had worked from 1974 to 1976, had had a series of rapid promotions and was now Under-Secretary in charge of International Relations. I arranged to meet him and registered my interest in the post. He said the decision would be for the Head of Branch, Peter Brannen, but he would inform him of my interest.

Part of my problem in not getting promotion had been that the "Powers That Be" were looking, on the whole, for go-getting management types to run organisations like the Training Agency and the Employment Services, whereas I was seen as a "Policy Principal". However, when it became known that I was looking for a move, it became apparent that there was a shortage of "Policy Principals" and I had two other offers of work. One was in the Health and Safety Executive, with the daunting task of drawing up the regulations implementing a large number of

European health and safety directives. I declined that, with thanks. Bob David was also in charge of the Small Firms Division of the Department. He asked me to go and see another head of branch and the latter almost persuaded me to take a job with him. By this time Peter Brannen had more or less offered me the job dealing with the ILO, when it became vacant, so out of politeness I went to tell him that I was proposing to take the other job. Peter persuaded me to think again, for which I am eternally grateful.

Meanwhile, in the rest of the world, rapid, and previously unthinkable, changes were taking place. The Berlin Wall came down and many countries of Central and Eastern Europe broke away from the Soviet bloc: Hungary, Poland, Czechoslovakia, East Germany, Romania and Bulgaria. The Minister of State in the Department of Employment, Timothy Eggar, asked the Department to explore whether we could help the newly independent countries in any way within the Department's area of competence. Bob David was instructed to examine the possibilities and report back within a tight time framework. He, or Peter Brannen, asked me if I would be interested in this job, which I was. At the same time, Michael Howard took over from Norman Fowler as Secretary of State. So, instead of moving to a backwater, I moved into the job in the Department which had the highest profile at my level! By this time Sir Geoffrey Holland had moved over from the MSC to become Permanent Secretary in the DE.

I was given an office in Steel House, opposite Caxton House in Tothill Street. Steel House was an old-fashioned building with metal windows. I was given an office, but no staff, no office furniture and no telephone extension. I had to negotiate every item of furniture, which, naturally, was in short supply at that time. I seem to recall that obtaining a waste paper basket was particularly difficult. Personal computers were just beginning to come into fashion, but I had not yet mastered word-processing.

(One weekend, early on, someone lent me a laptop, or the current equivalent. I carefully wrote out what I wanted to say in long-hand and then typed it up. However, I managed to lose all that I had written and did not try again until much later.)

Normally, at my level, all typing was sent to a typing pool, from which it emerged, usually with a large number of mistakes, a couple of days later. I made it clear that I could not operate in this way and so I was allowed to engage agency secretaries – at great expense to the Department. This, in itself, was a mixed blessing, because it meant I had to "train" a new secretary frequently. Fortunately, there was one who stayed quite a long time.

A "Know How Fund" had been set up jointly by the Foreign Office (FCO) and the Ministry of Overseas Development (ODM)) to help coordinate efforts, such as ours, to help the newly independent countries. I was to work closely with them. Some months later Barney Smith was appointed to be in charge of the Fund. I had met Barney on the ENA course in Paris in 1976. He had also come to work in UKREP just before I left. Later, Barney was HM Ambassador to Nepal and later still, HM Ambassador to Thailand.

In order to prepare the report, which I was charged with producing, I wrote to the British ambassadors in the countries potentially concerned: Poland, Hungary, Czechoslovakia, East Germany (DDR), Bulgaria and Romania. In discussions with the Minister, we had established that possible areas where we might help were: employment services, training, health and safety at work and assistance to small firms. Ambassadors were asked to sound out the governments to see, whether there was any potential for help in any of these areas.

I received substantive replies from all, except Czechoslovakia. Stuart Laing was the Deputy Ambassador in Prague. He was working in UKREP, during the first year or two that I was there, so I knew him. He wrote back and said that they were too busy to do what we asked, but if I wanted to go out there, he would arrange for me to meet the appropriate people. Accordingly, in the middle of February 1990, I flew to Prague, accompanied by John Temple from the Training Agency.

It is hard to appreciate, thirty years later, what an adventure this was. For all my life up to that point, Prague (and all the other Central and East European capitals) had been forbidden territory and, furthermore, somewhere that one did not particularly want to go to. The whole experience was extraordinary. During the drive from the airport in Prague, we passed scores of old dilapidated buildings, nearly all held up by scaffolding. In many cases there was more scaffolding holding up the original scaffolding. Then we would go into areas – around the Castle and the main square – with magnificent buildings that looked like illustrations from a child's fairy tale book. We went out for a meal in the evening. The cost for the two of us, including wine, was about £2. By contrast, we were staying in the Forum Hotel. One evening, John was not feeling very well and asked for a whisky: this was charged at highly inflated western prices!

A meeting was arranged with representatives of the Federal Ministry of Labour and Social Affairs on the morning after we arrived – a Thursday. We had no specific agenda. We went into a room, where there were half a dozen men seated, all senior officials in the Ministry, some of whom had survived from the Communist regime. This was probably the most productive meeting I ever had. The Czech and Slovak officials were very business-like, very pragmatic and very clear on what they wanted. After two hours we had established the framework of an agreement. After the meeting I sent a telegram to the Know How Fund telling them what we wanted to do. They were somewhat taken aback by the speed of events, but fully supportive of our initiative.

We visited a number of other official bodies in the next 24 hours, but these were not significant in terms of our main mission. We also went to a concert in the Prague Opera House. I did not understand a word of what was going on, but the building was magnificent.

On the Friday afternoon, the Ambassador, Mr Peter O'Keefe, took us for a meeting with the Minister, Petr Miller. Mr Miller was a blacksmith – like my father. But, unlike my father, he had been imprisoned by the Communist regime until a few months before. I do not usually notice men's eyes, but Mr Miller had intense blue eyes, which sent the message to me at least that here was a man that I could trust. I went over the things that we wanted to try to do and he was very appreciative.

A young (36 year-old) Czech official was at both the main meetings. His name is Milos Zdenek. After the meeting with Mr Miller, he approached John and me and asked whether we were staying in Prague on the Saturday. In those days airfares were cheaper, if there was a Saturday night between the outward and return flights. When we said that we were, he asked if we would like him to show us round the city, and did we mind if he brought his six-year-old daughter with him? So began a beautiful friendship: we met several times in the nineties in Brussels and Prague and more recently Milos and Jana have been to stay with us four times in Skegness.

Milos and I worked together on a Joint Statement to be signed by the two Governments. I think we corresponded by Fax, which was just coming into common use. I also arranged for a party of senior Czech and Slovak officials to visit the UK just before Easter. Milos came on this visit and we sat in my office and finalised the text of the Joint Statement. Michael Howard went out to Prague, accompanied by Bob David, to sign the Joint Statement on 14 May 1990. A record timetable for an international treaty? When Milos came to see me in 2019 he brought me a copy of the original Joint Statement signed by the two ministers. I have attached this as an Appendix.

Michael Howard took a keen personal interest in this work. Consequently I sent him long updates on what we were doing, almost daily. I wrote all these by hand and then had them typed up. I had meetings with Michael Howard about once a week. It was decided between us that we would try to help Poland, Hungary and Czechoslovakia initially. Accordingly, I arranged exploratory visits first to Poland and then to Hungary. These were more high-powered than my visit to Prague.

Bob David led the visit to Warsaw, accompanied by officials from the Employment Services Agency (Roger Lasko) Health and Safety (Peter Graham, who had been at UKREP) and Small Firms (Pam Buley), all of whom were senior to me. We went to Warsaw just before Easter. The prices in the shops were even lower than in Prague. Warsaw was a city of contrasts. It did not seem as rundown as Prague. Many of the buildings were uninspiring Stalinist edifices. The old town, however, was beautiful. It had been razed to the ground by the Nazis, but had been reconstructed, stone by stone from old drawings. We also visited a training centre in Łodz and spent the night there. Our Polish host, who had accompanied us from Warsaw explained how Poland had been squeezed, through the centuries by its two powerful neighbours. He declined to say which one he was most afraid of.

Following this visit I prepared a lengthy report on possible action. This led to Michael Howard visiting Warsaw to sign a Joint Statement with the Polish Minister of Labour, Jacek Kuron. The two men could not have been more different in character: Michael Howard was urbane and cerebral, whereas Jacek Kuron was earthy and rumbustious. However, they got on really well together: my last memory of them is, as we were in the car leaving the last meeting between the two men, of Mr Kuron running out of the house to give Mr Howard a last present.

During the last official meeting, it was agreed that I should stay behind in Warsaw to tie up some loose ends, the following day. This meant that I had a free afternoon. I decided to go into the Old Town. There was a big expensive looking café in a square near the centre. I decided to be extravagant and treat myself to a fresh orange juice, which I thought would be expensive. I ordered my orange juice and spent a long time, sitting in the June sunshine, savouring it. Eventually, I asked for the bill. It was 30 zlotys. The exchange rate at the time was 14,000 zlotys to the pound. I had only a 10,000 zloty note. The waitress spent about half an hour finding the change.

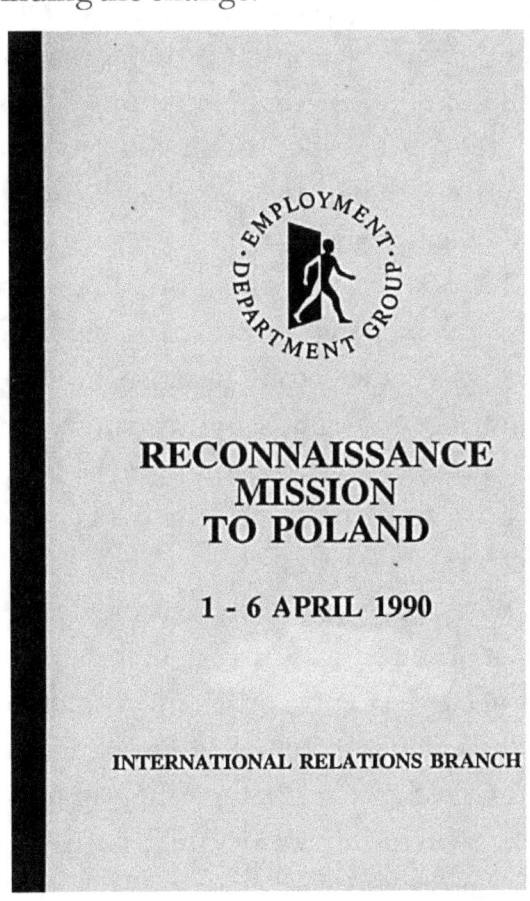

Soon after the first Polish visit, Peter Brannen led an exploratory mission to Hungary. While parts of Budapest were rundown and many prices were lower than in the UK, it was much more cosmopolitan than the other capitals I had been to. I remember thinking that the main (luxury) shopping street was not much different from Bond Street in London. The hotel we stayed in was on the banks of the Danube, looking up to the old town of Pest. That in itself is very beautiful. On a day off, Peter and I went on a boat trip up the Danube. On the boat were Peter Briers, Kenneth Brannagh and Emma Thompson. (Needless to say, it was Peter Brannen who recognised them, not me!) We went to a small town called Szentendre on an island near Budapest. It was very beautiful. A few months later, I accompanied Michael Howard to Budapest for a series of meetings, culminating in the signature of another Joint Statement. On the Sunday the Ambassador took us to the same island. My memory of that trip is of Michael Howard looking very relaxed, licking an ice-cream.

Following this political activity in the three countries a large number of bilateral exchanges were made between the UK and the three countries – actually four, because the Czech and Slovak services were autonomous. I was involved in co-ordinating these activities, but no longer involved in the visits. Nevertheless, the job remained busy and I rarely left the office much before the doors were locked at 8:00 pm.

During this period, I received all FCO telegrams relating to the situation in East and Central Europe, including discussions on the reunification of Germany and on the intractable situation in Kosovo. I also received information about available posts within and outside the Civil Service. On the Friday in July before I went on three weeks' leave, I took a note I had prepared for the Secretary of State over to Bob David. We had a light-hearted conversation, towards the end of which I said: "You realise I'm giving up all these interesting opportunities to work abroad, in order to continue to work for you, don't you?" Bob: "Which?" Me: "The Labour attaché post in Brussels, for a start." Bob: "Would you be interested in going back to Brussels?" Me: "Yes." When I got back to the office three weeks' later, there was a message for me to go and see Peter Brannen immediately. Peter told me that it had been arranged for me to go to work in the European Commission: Michael Howard had been consulted and agreed.

Brussels 2

The European Commission Building – *Le Berlaymont* – before refurbishment

Of course, it wasn't as simple as that. What had actually happened was that Keith Masson, my successor's successor in UKREP, had had a conversation with Herman van Zonneveld, who was head of the Employment Law Division in the Commission. Herman had said that he was short of staff and he would be interested in having a National Expert. Keith had reported this back to London and they had interpreted it as a definite offer. Be that as it may, one rainy October day, I arrived in Brussels, for the first time for about six years. I immediately succumbed again to its charm. I had a good discussion with Herman van Zonneveld, and, after a few more hiccups, I started work on the 21st January 1991.

Before I left London, I was summoned to see Michael Forsyth, who was a Eurosceptic junior minister in the Department of Employment. He asked me whether he should measure in days or hours the length of time it would take me to "go native". He added that it had taken Leon Brittan – a former Conservative cabinet minister, who was now a Vice-President of the Commission – about a week to go native. Michael Howard also sent me a note via his Private Secretary, wishing me well, thanking me for all the work I had done and saying that I would be "sorely missed".

The transition was not nearly as straightforward as it had been the first time round, though we had the advantage of knowing about banks, the best areas to live and the transport system – though the metro system had expanded considerably since we last lived there. Around New Year we went to spend a week staying with our friends Syd and Wendy Allman in order to open bank accounts and find somewhere to live. We hadn't factored in the New Year Public Holiday, so, effectively, we had two full days to look for accommodation. We looked at 17 or 18 houses in that time, with three different agencies. It was dark when we saw the last two or three houses on the Thursday afternoon. We were driven back to the agency in Watermael-Boitsfort and the agent put us under pressure to sign up for one of the properties. We were tired and, in any case, I was not going to sign up without sleeping on it. Eventually we were released from her "prison", with the promise that we would go back and look at the property we thought we liked the best in the morning. We were still in bed at 9:00 the following morning, when the agency rang to say that the landlord had agreed to reduce the rent by 3000 Belgian francs (about £50) a month. We made an appointment to meet the agency and decided to take the property. We made a good choice: of all the houses that I have lived in that was the one that I liked best.

Before we moved in we were advised to have an expert report undertaken about the state of the property, so that we would be able to show, when we left, what was already wrong with the property before we moved in. Syd and Wendy's son, Max, joined me to show the expert round. Max pointed out that there was no pole to open the trapdoor to the loft. The expert turned on him and said: *Il n'y a pas d'éléphants non plus!* There aren't any elephants either – "I say what is there, not what isn't there".

Before we went to look at property we had gone to the BBL (Banque Bruxelles Lambert) to open two accounts. The first was a joint account and the second was in Jennifer's name. Other married women said they had had problems opening a bank account, but on this occasion, it went ahead without a hitch. It was important for a married woman to have her own account, because, if the husband were to die, the joint account would be immediately frozen. The women used to say to each other: "If your husband dies, go to the bank and draw all the money out, before you register the death!"

We also had to re-import the car, which we had bought in Belgium ten years earlier. We had to get Belgian identity cards and register with a social security *mutuelle* for health care and open accounts with the electricity and fuel companies. We received some help with all this from the Commission, but last time round, most of this had been done by the Representation.

I stayed with Syd and Wendy for the first few weeks, before Jennifer came out in mid-February. I went back to England for a few days. It was minus 14 in Brussels and there were heavy snowfalls in London. It took me an age to get from Heathrow to Watford. There was still a lot of snow on the ground, when we left Watford, a few days later to get the overnight ferry from Felixstowe, so we left early in order to get there in the daylight.

All our goods and chattels had been loaded into a furniture van by a local Watford removal company a few days earlier. Included was a large heavy chest of drawers, which had been kept in one of the upstairs bedrooms. The removal people had taken all the drawers out and carried them and the shell downstairs separately; then they had loaded them on to the removal lorry, where they put the drawers and their contents back into the shell for the journey. There was still snow on the ground when our belongings arrived at our new house in Brussels in a 'Pickfords' lorry.

The new house was on three floors. The entrance was on the ground floor, where there was also a garage, a bedroom and a number of smaller rooms and cupboards. On the first floor there was only a very large 'J' shaped living room and a smallish kitchen.

The living room t 80 Rue Sombre, Woluwe St. Pierre, Woluwe

There were three more bedrooms, a bathroom and toilet on the second floor. There was a beautiful wooden winding staircase linking the three floors. We had decided that we wanted the chest of drawers in the small bedroom on the second floor. So the two muscular Flemish removal men decided to lift the chest of drawers out of the lorry and carry it up two flights of stairs. Three-quarters of the way up, they stopped to complain that it was heavy! They hadn't thought to take the drawers out!

With the Commission's help, I managed to get Belgian number plates for the car without any problem. I expected to get a letter from the Belgian authorities requiring me to take the car to the *Contrôle Technique* (the equivalent of the MOT in the UK) but I didn't receive one. I came to realise that it was illegal to drive a car that did not have a valid certificate. It was July or August before I tried to do anything about it. I had found a garage round the corner and the owner had said he would take the car for me. However, he came back to me and said there were major problems and I would have to go myself. The least of these problems was that part of the bodywork was rusty and, along with other similar problems, that would need attention before they could issue a certificate.

The first major problem was that I needed to produce the previous certificate. When I said that I didn't have one, they said that it was impossible to register a car without a certificate. It took some time to persuade them that I had in fact managed to register the car without going to the *Contrôle Technique*. The really difficult problem was that the chassis number on all the paper work was different from the one stamped on the engine of the car. This had not been a problem in England, because, when we imported it into England, the number had been copied from the engine. However, as I had bought the car in Belgium, I still had the original document with a different number on it. The garage where I bought the car had since moved to Waterloo. I had to go back there to get the paperwork changed, or so I thought.

It was a French car and by this time it was August and most of the French were on holiday. However, they were eventually able to check the paperwork, only to find that the correct number was on the paperwork and it was the number on the chassis that was wrong! It is a criminal offence to alter the chassis number on a car without judicial authority. Eventually, I had to take the car back to the Peugeot garage for them to delete the old number and stamp in a new one – and to give me a paper to say that it had been done in *bonne et due forme*. I then had to go back to the *Contrôle Technique* for the third or fourth time – each time it took ages to get into the place without the proper papers – and they eventually gave me a certificate. In all the fuss, they forgot about the problems with the bodywork etc.!

As a National Expert I had no status in the Commission and so I expected to have a fairly easy time. That was the case initially, but things changed gradually, until, at the end I was working as many hours as I had been in London. Herman's unit was responsible for making most of the proposals under the Commission's Social Action Programme, which had been drawn up under the direction of Jacques Delors, who had been President of the Commission since 1985. The programme included proposals for directives on working time, part time work, temporary work, works councils, young workers and detached workers. It also promised a Commission Opinion on an Equitable Wage. To my surprise, Herman asked me if I would take on the Working Time Directive. This had already been drafted by Klaus Käding, who had since left the unit. The proposal had met with strong opposition from the British Government, in the person of Michael Howard. Herman also had joint responsibility, with John Morley's unit, for the Commission Opinion on an Equitable Wage. I was given that as well.

By the time I arrived, the proposal for a Working Time Directive had almost completed its first reading in the European Parliament and in the Economic and Social Committee. One of my first tasks was to draft the Commission's response to the Parliament's Opinion and to draft a revised proposal taking into account those of the Parliament's amendments which the Commission wished to accept. Treaty changes, made since I was in Brussels before, meant that the Parliament had a much more important role in the preparation of legislation than it had previously. Directives were now the joint responsibility of the Council of Ministers and the European Parliament. So, the Commission's revised proposal went to the Social Questions Group for the Council to adopt, not a Directive, as it would have done eight years before, but a Common Position, which would then be sent for debate in Parliament. I accompanied Herman to the meetings of the Social Questions Group, but, unlike ten years before when I had been President of the Group, I was not allowed to speak. I was, however, fully involved in the Commission's negotiating position – not that there was that much room for manoeuvre.

In truth, the Commission's original proposal was a pretty tame affair. Crucially, it said nothing about limiting the number of hours that could be worked weekly. The French, at least since 1936, have been obsessed by working time. They said that they would not agree to a Directive which did not have a limit on the weekly hours of work. Eventually an amendment emerged with a maximum working week of 48 hours.

Other important issues which were raised included the many circumstances under which "derogations" could be allowed – to cater for situations, where it would not be practical to apply the rules of the Directive strictly. In certain cases, it was argued, successfully, that the nature of the work was so different that it would not be possible to apply the rules of the Directive at all. Eventually, all transport activities along with offshore work, sea fishing and doctors in training were excluded from the Directive, but each of these exclusions was the subject of many hours of difficult negotiation, before it was conceded. The Commission, in the person of Jean Degimbe, my Director-General, had a statement put in the Council minutes to the effect that the Commission would bring forward proposals for regulating working time in respect of each of the sectors and activities excluded from the Directive.

A third principal bone of contention was a German amendment to the effect that the weekly rest day should, in principle, be a Sunday. This last proposal brought me quite a number of lunch invitations. I think I would have been scrupulous anyway, but their money was wasted, because I was not in a position to influence events, if I had wanted to. At the same time, the debate over the opening of shops on Sundays in England and Wales was raging and both sides in the argument came to lobby me. Similarly, the organisation responsible for offshore work in the UK lobbied me regularly for its exclusion.

The proposal lost momentum during 1992, but was picked up again in 1993 by the Danish Presidency. The Council reached a Common Position in June 1993 in Luxembourg. The Common Position then went to the European Parliament for a second reading. The *rapporteur* this time round was Stephen Hughes, a British Labour MEP. The Parliament's Social Affairs Committee had decided to hold a meeting in Thessaloniki in Greece. I was still not allowed to speak on behalf of the Commission, so my future boss, Rosendo Gonzalez Dorrego went with me. Stephen Hughes was a pragmatist and he steered the Directive through the Parliament. It was finally adopted on 4 November 1993.

The Commission Opinion on an Equitable Wage made equally slow progress, but was adopted by the Commission on 1 September 1993 (COM(93) 388 final). Pádraig Flynn was appointed as Commissioner for Employment and Social Affairs in early 1993. He was an Irish conservative. The European Parliament decided to discuss the Commission Opinion at its plenary meeting in Strasbourg, soon after he had been appointed. I had to provide a written brief and a draft speech. I also had to go to Strasbourg for an oral briefing. It was the first time Mr Flynn had met me and several other Commission officials. He was a very tall man with broad shoulders and an impressive presence. I was particularly impressed by the fact that he took two or three minutes to talk about me and where I came from. He then asked me what this "socialist nonsense" was all about. My speech of several pages was reduced to half a page. When it came to the discussion in Parliament, Mr Flynn read it beautifully and gave the impression that this Opinion was dear to his heart and he had spent a lifetime working on it!

A Royal Invitation

Towards the end of 1991, my first year in the Commission, I was sitting at my desk, when I received a strange telephone call. A very posh sounding lady by the name of Patsy Knight said she was ringing from the Prince of Wales' office in Windsor Castle. Sir Geoffrey Holland, the Permanent Secretary of the Department of Employment, had given her my name. Her story was so surreal that at first I thought it was some sort of practical joke. But it wasn't. Every year the Prince arranged for a group of "young" people who would be the next generation of "movers and shakers" across the political spectrum to get together to exchange ideas and establish a network. I was neither young (aged 52) nor a high-flyer, but she was looking for someone to bring a European perspective. I accepted the invitation. Other people at Windsor Castle with me included Jenny Abramsky, who was already high up in the BBC hierarchy. She was called away after a couple of hours. Claude Moraes, who became a senior Labour Member of the European Parliament was also there. Then there was Rachel Squire, who was elected as Labour MP for Dunfermline West at the 1992 election. Rachel was a very modest person, but reputably a very good and popular constituency MP. She was on the Defence Select Committee and came to stay with us several times, when the Committee came to Brussels. Unfortunately she died prematurely in 2006.

Staying in Brussels?

Towards the end of 1993, my secondment from the Department of Employment was coming to an end. The Commission were keen for me to stay and there was a possibility that I might be able to get a one-year contract from the Commission as an "auxiliary". As ever, there was no guarantee that I would be appointed before my secondment came to an end. This put me in a quandary. There were three possibilities. The first was that I went back to the Department of Employment. If I took the job with the Commission, assuming it materialised, there were two options with regard to my Civil Service pension. Either I could freeze it and take an actuarially reduced pension at the age of sixty, or I could pay voluntary contributions for the further year that I remained with the Commission. Neither of these was at all attractive.

I had several conversations with the Personnel Officer in the Department, but the early ones were not at all productive. I then telephoned him on a Thursday round about my birthday in

November. He asked me what I wanted to do and I repeated that none of the options were appealing. He asked about early retirement and I said that I wasn't interested under the terms that they could offer. He then said that they were looking for volunteers for redundancy. If I was interested, I would need to let him know by the following Monday. Of course, there was absolutely no guarantee, or even a probability, that I would be offered anything after the year as an auxiliary expired – and that contract could not be extended – but I decided to accept the offer. So, in January 1994, at the age of 54, I became a Civil Service Pensioner, with the same pension as I would have received, if I had carried on until I was 60.

***

I was of particular value to the Commission, because I was one of the few people in DGV who was a native English speaker and who could write good English. John Morley and later his colleague, Danny Brennan, were the others. Herman van Zonneveld's unit was the most high-profile unit in the Directorate-General and the Commissioner, who in the early years was Greek, and the Director-General, who was Belgian, often had to make speeches in English. In addition, John Morley and I were the only ones with a British Civil Service background of briefing ministers and by this time I was rather good at it.

These qualities became even more important when Pádraig Flynn took over as Commissioner. In the early days I did a lot of briefing for him and I got the impression that I was one of the few people in the Directorate-General, whose advice he trusted – I never flattered or told people what I thought they wanted to hear, but I had a pretty good sense of what was politically possible or necessary.

By that time Hywel Jones had come back to DGV, first as Deputy-Director-General and then, almost immediately on the retirement of Jean Degimbe, as Acting Director-General. Towards the end of 1994, relations between him and John Morley had become strained and he asked me, through his assistant, Sarah Evans, to take a new job coordinating speech-writing. I was uneasy about this, but felt it would be difficult to refuse, especially as, by this time, I was looking to get a new contract, as a temporary agent, for which I would need Hywel Jones' support. I talked it over with Jennifer who advised that, at my age, I should not do anything I was uncomfortable with. I went back to Sarah Evans and told her. I asked, if it would make any difference to my contract and she assured me that Mr Jones would be disappointed, but that it wouldn't make any difference – and to be fair, it didn't.

Obtaining the contract as a temporary agent was fraught with difficulties. Traditionally there was an age limit of 55 for new recruits, which would have excluded me. However, the UKREP and the DGV argued successfully that the age limit should be removed, because the European Union (EU) was developing a policy of non-discrimination against older workers. This was going against the trend in many countries of offering employees early retirement in order to avoid redundancies – the very policy which I had benefited from a year earlier. I managed to line up in support of my application the UKREP, the Irish cabinet (Pádraig Flynn), Hywel Jones and both the CBI and TUC representatives in Brussels.

I was supposed to fly through the interview, which I was doing until a Trade Union representative asked me some questions about the European Parliament. First of all I made the mistake of being rather dismissive about the parliament's importance and then he asked me how many British Labour MEPs there were.

That is the sort of detail that I have never considered particularly important. I began to waffle, but, fortunately, Sarah Evans, who was on the panel, helped me out. The panel approved my appointment, but it then had to go through a process, which involved the trade union representatives. Scurrilous articles appeared in informal in-house publications, about this retired British civil servant who was trying to take a job, which could have been done by a younger person. I managed to counter this argument by pointing out that I had actually been made compulsorily redundant by the British Government. I was becoming anxious by this time, so, when my appointment was finally agreed, I pressed to start as early as possible. I re-joined the Commission on 1 November 1995, nine months after my previous contract had ended. It was also two days before my 56th birthday. That potentially was a big mistake, to which I will return later.

From about 1993, with Herman van Zonneveld, I got involved with studying the relationship between flexibility, security and employment and I ran a series of small study groups to examine aspects of this. While I was "unemployed" I wrote a paper for the Commission on this subject. The related issue of Work Organisation featured prominently in Jacques Delors' White Paper on *Growth, Competitiveness and Employment*, which was the most important document, produced during his period as President of the Commission. Although my former colleague, Lars-Erik Andreassen was the expert on Work Organisation, responsibility for taking that matter forward was transferred back to Herman van Zonneveld and delegated to me.

Japanese interludes

Not for the first time in my career, there was a "turf war" between one of my bosses and her counterpart in another part of the organisation. On this occasion it was between my relatively new Director, Odile Quintin, who was in charge of industrial relations, and Karl-Johann Lönnroth, the Finnish Director responsible for Employment Policy. There were regular conferences between Europe and Japan, involving the European Commission, the Japanese Ministry of Labour and representatives of employers and workers on both sides. In 1996, the Conference was to be held in Tokyo and the theme was "New Patterns of Work". Odile Quintin didn't want to go, but she didn't want another Director to go either.

After a period of wrangling, in which I took no part, it was decided that I should go, much to the chagrin of the other Directors, who wanted this perk. I went as one of the two keynote speakers from the European side – the other was Gerhard Bosch from the *Institut für Arbeit und Technik* in Gelsenkirchen. The Commission team consisted of Hywel Jones, who was still Acting Director-General, accompanied by Fay Devonic, who was head of the international unit, and me.

This was one of the highlights of my career. I had never been to Asia before. We were supposed to fly with SABENA, the Belgian airline, in Business Class. Fay Devonic made a mistake with the booking – she should have got a reduced rate. To compensate, we were put in 'J' class (almost First Class) and travelled in the same compartment as the King of the Belgians had travelled the previous week. There were about ten large well-padded reclining seats in the compartment. A steward took our coats as soon as we arrived and offered us drinks, whenever we wanted them: a luxurious experience, far removed from the Economy Class that

I was used to! (Hywel Jones, who had booked separately, went in Business Class, much to his annoyance!)

We arrived in Japan on a Saturday morning in October. We stayed at the Intercontinental Hotel. In the early afternoon, the three of us went for a walk. I was overwhelmed by the fact that I could not read anything that was written on street or other "information" signs. The nearest railway and underground station was Shinjuku, which had about 60 exits and entrances. We walked past one of these and were impressed by the thousands of people pouring out of the station.

Japanese bedroom (with Welsh quilt) Zushi, 27 October 1996

Hywel Jones had been in contact with a former girlfriend who was married to a Japanese man and lived in Yokohama on the Pacific coast. We decided to go and visit her on the Sunday morning. We had to travel by train from Shinjuku, changing twice. The first problem was buying train tickets. We spent a long time trying to buy tickets from a machine. Eventually we discovered that the machine belonged to a different railway company from the one we needed. We made the journey without major problems and were fortunate to be able to see inside a Japanese house.

Tokyo Conference, 1 November 1996

The conference went very well. Again we were fortunate to get under the surface of life in Japan. All the people we met were very courteous and, within strict limits, quite open about their problems and policies for dealing with them.

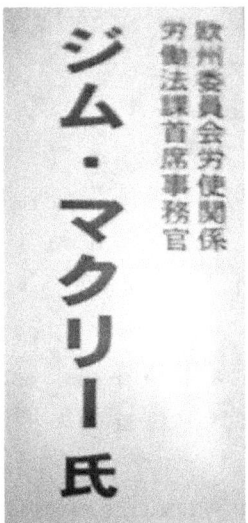

My name sheet at the Conference

In 'J' class – the journey home – Fay Devonic and me

It came to pass that I had two further dealings with the Japanese. In early 2000 another Conference was arranged in Tokyo. This time, I was asked to go as an expert. (I can't remember what I was supposed to be an expert on.) This time we travelled in Business Class, which was far less exotic. We again had a free day on the Sunday – it was in the days when with a (cheaper) APEX ticket, the stay had to include a Saturday night.

On the Sunday morning I decided to walk in the opposite direction to the one I'd taken in 1996. I walked to a park. I remember noting that there seemed to be more 'down and outs' than there had been the last time. In this park there was a Shinto temple, which I wanted to look at. When I got there I was told politely but firmly that I couldn't go in, because a wedding ceremony was about to begin. I stood at a discreet distance from the entrance – alongside a Japanese couple - to watch the people arrive. To my surprise, when all the guests were installed, the doorkeeper gestured to the Japanese couple and then to me to step inside and sit at the back, having, of course, first taken our shoes off. The ceremony consisted of a man intoning ritual formulae, interspersed with the beating of cymbals or other instruments. Afterwards the guests gathered outside for photographs. The bride's mother and attendants had incredibly beautiful dresses. The bride wore a white dress. She had dark spiky hair with what looked like rollers at the end of each spike – not particularly attractive! The bridegroom's uncle invited me to join the party. He was saying that traditional Shinto weddings were fairly rare. Then I was invited to have my photograph taken with the bride. It being Japan, that meant quite a lot of photos. I have to admit that the bride did not seem particularly impressed or interested, but I was told afterwards that it was considered to be lucky to have a Caucasian at one's wedding.

Japanese wedding, February 2000

The Conference again went smoothly, along similar lines to the previous one, except that, as an 'expert' my speech was much shorter. At the end of the Conference I learned that the plane that I was due to fly back on was overbooked. Somehow I was the unfortunate (!) one who was selected to stay in Japan for an extra two nights. I took advantage of my free day to go on an excursion to Mount Fuji, which was very impressive. We were about 40 kilometres out of Tokyo, when we stopped in a huge carpark by a shopping centre for a 'comfort' break. We had got back into the coach and the coach was driving off, when two women were spotted in the carpark, frantically waving their arms. Not the best place to be left stranded!

My final involvement with the Japanese was in 2002. By then I had retired. A few days after my father had died, I received a phone call from a former colleague, Tony Lockett, to ask if I would write the report for a Japanese visit to Brussels in the spring. I did this, so my progress with the Japanese was from Keynote Speaker to Expert to Secretary!

Back to the real world

The new Director-General in 1996 was Allan Larsson. Allan was an economist and a former Swedish Trade Unionist. In my experience the Swedish Trade Unions were the most progressive in Europe. Allan was a pragmatist and believed passionately in the need for a different, more participative, less confrontational approach to the organisation of work. He persuaded the Commission to accept the idea of producing a Green Paper (i.e. a discussion document) on work organisation. I was charged with producing this document. I was going to say "writing" this document. In fact I typed it on my computer, but Allan wrote most of it. In the autumn of 1997 the Commission published its Green Paper: *Partnership for a new organization of work*.

As an aside, Allan was passionate about the need to adapt to technological change, rather than to fight against it. He pointed out that if there had been no technological change over the previous generation, in order to sustain current levels of telephone communication, the whole population of Sweden would have to employed as telephone operators – and that was before the internet had really taken hold!

Allan and I spent a lot of time, mostly separately, travelling round Europe, discussing the Green Paper at conferences organised variously by employer and trade union organisations – occasionally jointly. In particular I remember going to Stockholm, Copenhagen, London, Dublin, Helsinki and Bonn. I also went to Lisbon in the following year.

Taken during my visit to Helsinki!

The Irish took the Green Paper very seriously and at the time transformed their industrial relations arrangements nationally from a backward-looking confrontational style to a new approach based on partnership. At the Conference in Dublin, Pádraig Flynn was the main speaker. I also spoke. Mr Flynn at the beginning of his talk said that he disliked speaking at the same event as one of his officials, because the official wrote both speeches (which was true) but kept the best bits for themselves. In this case I don't think that was true.

The most interesting Conference was organised in Bonn by the German employers' organisation (BDA). Allan Larsson was supposed to be the main Commission representative, but had to send his apologies to say that he would arrive only in the afternoon. So I was the only Commission representative. The BDA were hostile to the Green Paper, not because of its content, but because they suspected (I think wrongly on this occasion) that the Commission wanted to start interfering in matters, which, in Germany, were nothing to do with Government and *a fortiori* nothing to do with the European Commission. Speaker after speaker expressed their hostility in no uncertain terms. When I am not being attacked personally, I don't feel uncomfortable in these situations. I can't remember what I said or did, but I look back on the experience with amusement rather than humiliation. The hostility was intensified in the afternoon, but Allan Larsson had been a politician and he was more than capable of standing up for himself. There were two postscripts to this. Around Christmas, a very large parcel arrived in my office: a case of German wine with the compliments of the BDA! A few months later I was at a meeting in Brussels and a German (not from the BDA!) came up to me and apologised for the unforgiveable rudeness of his compatriots!

At about the same time Pádraig Flynn was invited to a meeting in Dublin with the top men in multinational firms in Ireland – IBM etc. – about his proposal for a Works Council Directive. His office persuaded them that it would be better if one of the officials from the unit responsible for it went to talk to them first. Despite the fact that I had never really understood it, nor had much sympathy for it, I was delegated to go. I was invited to meet them for breakfast and then talk to them about the Directive in a meeting afterwards. As I had expected, they were not very keen on the proposal and they asked me a lot of searching questions. I do remember thinking how kind and polite they had been throughout. I certainly didn't feel as though I had been given a grilling. Afterwards the organiser asked me if I liked whiskey. I said that I did. He said that, as they had given me such a "rough time", they wanted to buy me a bottle of Middletons, but they didn't want to waste their money, if I didn't like it. They would send me a bottle. I had completely forgotten about this, but a few months later, I was working late one evening (as usual) when the evening porter rang me to say that there was a man in reception asking to see me. I went down and he gave me a bottle of Middletons – a numbered bottle, to be registered in my name. It is the most beautiful whiskey I have ever tasted. So much so that, several years later, I was in Dublin airport and I bought another one at a cost of 50 Irish pounds.

As I mentioned before, in the early nineties, when the Working Time Directive was being discussed in COREPER, it was agreed that various sectors and activities would be excluded from the Directive. At the time Jean Degimbe, our Director-General, placed on record in the minutes of COREPER that the Commission would bring forward proposals in respect of each of the sectors and activities excluded. I don't know whether anyone else would have remembered this, but I did and drew it to the attention of Pádraig Flynn. Sometime later Mr Flynn invited our Director-General, Allan Larsson, and my Director, Odile Quintin, and officials from our unit to a meeting to discuss the work programme for the year. At the preparatory meeting the night before, everyone in the room thought it would be a bad idea to make proposals on working time. I said that, nevertheless, I thought that was what Mr Flynn would want to do. I was instructed to write a note setting out the arguments against, which I did. However, Mr Flynn, as I had predicted, wanted to go ahead with proposals on working time.

Over the years since the Working Time Directive was adopted, negotiations had been ongoing in most of the excluded sectors in the Commission's Joint Industrial Committees. These covered: road transport, rail transport, sea transport, inland waterways and sea fishing. I took part in all these discussions. In addition the Commission had studies made of the situation in respect of offshore work and doctors in training.

The Commission decided to produce a package of arrangements for dealing with each of the excluded sectors and activities. I was instructed to draft the umbrella proposal amending the Working Time Directive. This I did by removing all the exclusions and then allowing specific provisions in respect of each activity. I have described elsewhere the painstakingly thorough process that was gone through when the Sex Discrimination Bill was drawn up in the UK some twenty years earlier – though I suspect that the process is not nearly as thorough nowadays. In this case, however, I drafted a proposal on my word processor and it went through the Commission relatively unscathed.

It then had to go through the European Parliament and the Council of Ministers. On this occasion I was the main Commission representative at most of the meetings. I had retained my ability to produce constructive compromises and I believe I was helpful in solving the many difficult issues that arose in the course of the long negotiations. The *rapporteur* for the European Parliament this time round was Michel Rocard, a former French Prime Minister and, in my opinion, one of the best. During the Committee stages, I was the person responsible for answering his queries. I have to say that he was always very polite and gentle towards me.

The Directive was finally adopted just before I left Brussels - on 22 June 2000.

A few years before I retired, the Commission introduced a new staff appraisal system. In order to avoid the common practice of nearly everyone being given top marks, each Directorate and unit was given an aggregate total of the marks to be allocated (something like 24 per member of staff). The top mark was 33; anything below 16 required "action". By this time I was the only non-lawyer in our unit, which was mainly a law-making unit. I was also one of the few, who were not fully-fledged *fonctionnaires.* Consequently, I think I always had a slight sense of inferiority. I was pleased and surprised, therefore, when Rosendo Gonzalez Dorrego, who, by this time, had been promoted to be my head of unit, came to me to discuss the markings. He said: *of course you are the best,* but I would like to ask you to give up a couple of marks to give to someone whom we want to promote (bearing in mind that at that stage I was not looking for promotion).

Rosendo and me, October 1999

My initial contract as a temporary agent began on 1st November 1995. It was made abundantly clear at the time that I (and other people who were appointed in the same batch) could not expect the contract to be extended, nor could we expect to have favourable treatment to enable us to become fully-fledged *fonctionnaires.* (Previous practice had been to extend contracts to five years and then hold a limited competition for establishment as a *fonctionnaire.*) In the course of 1998, the year when my contract was due to expire, representations were made on behalf of all temporary agents and the Commission finally agreed to allow extensions for another year to allow time to organise a new competition. This extension would take me up to 31st October 1999 – 3 days before my 60th birthday.

Relaxing with colleagues at Rosendo's house

Rosendo Gonzalez Dorrego, me, Franz Burger and Gertrud Feustel

Franz Burger, Rosendo Gonzalez Dorrego and Fernando Vasquez

I had discovered at an induction meeting, when I became a temporary agent, that the qualification for a Commission retirement pension was as follows: either 10 years' service as a *fonctionnaire* or temporary agent; or reaching the age of sixty before retirement. I was going to be 3 days' short! The monetary value of the pension was considerably better than the modest 'redundancy' pay that I would receive as a temporary agent under 60. But the pension scheme also brought with it lifelong coverage under the Commission's medical scheme, which provides worldwide coverage for the retired person and to some extent their spouse. This would have been particularly important, because, at that time, we were planning to go to live in France. In the course of 1999, I tried hard to get an extension for a few days. Everyone was sympathetic, but "The Powers That Be" were adamant that they could not make an exception for me, because it would create a precedent.

The only possibility was to take and succeed in the competition to become a *fonctionnaire*. This was a tough competition, involving a lot of preparatory work – and knowledge. The success rate was about 25%. As usual, there was a dispute between the Commission and the staff unions, which resulted in a long delay in the holding of this competition. I decided to apply. August in the Commission is almost dead. I remember spending a warm afternoon in August 1999 filling in the long and detailed application form and wondering why I was bothering, as I had no intention of taking the examination. In mid-August we started to make firm plans to move to Antibes. At the end of August, my father, who was 87 at the time, was knocked down by a car and badly injured. He lived in Skegness. I, or we, travelled to Skegness from Brussels most weekends to see him. We already owned a property in Skegness and we decided very quickly to give notice to the tenants, with a view to moving there in December. By October, we had given notice to the landlord to leave our house in Brussels and Jennifer had given notice to leave her job at the International School in Brussels.

Round about the second weekend in October, I went on my own to spend a few days in Skegness with my father. On the Monday I went into the town centre. When I got back, my father said that he had received a telephone call from "a foreign gentleman". I managed to get back to him: it was the man in the Directorate responsible for personnel matters. He asked if I had applied for the competition to become a *fonctionnaire*. I said that I had, but I was going to withdraw. (This was on my 'to do' list!) He asked if I would be interested in staying on until the results of the competition were announced. The problem was that the Commission relied on temporary agents to man many areas of activity; the competition had been delayed yet again and in the meantime these posts would be vacant. I had to speak to the owner of our house in Brussels. Fortunately, he had been unable to let the house, so we were able to stay on. Interviews had already been held at the International School to fill Jennifer's post, but they agreed to keep her on for the time being. The outcome was that I stayed in post over the winter and I gave notice to retire on 30th June – with a pension and medical cover.

Important People

In the course of my career, I met a number a number of important people, many of whom I have mentioned above.

The Queen came to Brussels in the early 1980s. The staff of UKREP along with our spouses were summoned to the British Ambassador's residence, which was then situated near the centre of Brussels, overlooking the Park. We had to be there some forty minutes before the Queen was due to arrive and were lined up around the room. When the Queen arrived, she went one way round the room, while the Duke of Edinburgh went round the other way. He asked me a searching question about what Europe was doing about unemployment, to which I replied that the European Social Fund was designed to alleviate the effects of unemployment. He then went on to speak to Rob Hubbard. Rob's wife, Caroline, was a First Secretary, seconded from the Treasury. Prince Philip asked Rob what he did. He said he was a teacher at the British School of Brussels. When the Duke asked: *What are you doing here then?* Rob replied: *Just following the missus around!* The Duke muttered words to the effect *I know what you mean!*

I met the Prime Minister of Swaziland and two future Prime Ministers of Luxembourg and Presidents of the European Commission – Jacques Santer and Jean-Claude Juncker. I never got very close to a British Prime Minister. I went to a Labour Party rally in Birmingham just before the 1964 General Election, at which Roy Jenkins introduced Harold Wilson as "The next Prime Minister". I also went to a Conference about the employment of disabled people at the Queen Elizabeth Hall in Westminster, which James Callaghan addressed. I listened in on Edward Heath's conversation with Maurice Macmillan reported above. And I worked closely with Michael Howard, who was leader of the Conservative Party for a time, but never became Prime Minister.

I had more contact with future and past French Prime Ministers. I have already mentioned my dealings with Michel Rocard on the amendment of the Working Time Directive. Much earlier, 1982 or 1983, I went to a meeting of the Council of Ministers in Luxembourg. The reform of the European Social Fund was on the agenda. This was a very sensitive issue, because it involved the potential transfer of considerable sums of money from net contributors to the Community budget in favour of net beneficiaries. The President decided that the discussion should be restricted to Ministers plus one official. I was excluded from this discussion. At one point I decided to go to the toilet. While I was there the French Minister, Pierre Bérégovoy, came in. I asked him how things were going in the meeting. As I had expected, his answer was non-committal, but he seemed ready to enter into a conversation. He had previously been President Mitterrand's Secretary-General and he asked me if I knew his friend, Robert Armstrong, who, as Secretary to the Cabinet, had been his British counterpart at that time. Needless to say, I didn't know him, as Robert Armstrong was many places higher in the hierarchy than I was. Pierre Bérégovoy later became Prime Minister from April 1992 to March 1993.

What did I achieve in nearly 40 years?

My special subject at University had been the existentialist writers Sartre, Camus, Malraux and particularly St Exupéry. I don't think I was ever influenced very much by Sartre, other than to find him repugnant, but I was probably influenced subconsciously by St Exupéry. As a gross simplification, his philosophy boiled down to the need of individuals to give a meaning to their existence through their own actions and the influence their actions had on other people. My achievements as a civil servant can be measured against these two criteria.

In the grand scheme of things, I did not achieve a great deal. One of Malraux's heroes wanted to leave a scar on this world: *Je veux laisser une cicatrice sur cette terre.*[25] I certainly didn't do that, nor did I want to. I was not a Hitler nor a Stalin. Nor was I an Einstein or a Pasteur. Until the tragedy of Brexit[26], the United Kingdom Government and European Union were forces for peace and harmony in the world. Although there were many aberrations and inefficiencies, their well-functioning machinery of government was a vital component in the cohesion of society. The Civil Service is responsible for ensuring that the machine works and (it is to be hoped) continues to improve. Each civil servant is a cog in that machine. It is not glamourous, but it is essential.

Was I ever more than just a cog in the wheel? For the most part, the answer is probably: "No, but I was a well-tuned, piece of machinery". But, there were a number of occasions when I was more than that. I am particularly proud of the work I did on Eastern Europe. No doubt if someone else had been there they would have done a good job, but I do believe that I had the right

---

[25] André Malraux: *La Voie Royale* (Perken).
[26] I have included my 2016 essay: *Brexit: A Tragedy?* as an Annex to this book.

combination of experience, international outlook and resourcefulness to do an outstanding job. I often have difficulties working when I feel constrained by rules that I don't fully understand: in this job, there were no rules. Although it would be arrogant to suggest that I made a huge difference, I do think I played a small role in smoothing the transition from a planned economy to a market economy in Czechoslovakia and Poland. I don't think I could say the same about Hungary, where I was less involved personally and the other people involved on both sides were more complicated.

I also think I did a better job than most would have done in Swaziland, though not until Bob Thomas had given me a blueprint to follow. There I developed a coherent education and training policy, which I "sold" to the Swaziland Government of the day. In that case, however, I had no lasting influence, because the policies changed a few months later, following a mini coup.

The six months I spent as Chairman of the Social Questions Working Group in Brussels tell a similar story. It was certainly the most prestigious post I held and one which I fulfilled effectively and with imagination. I certainly enjoyed it and look back on it with pride. However, the actual achievements were negligible. I also broke new ground in setting up the regional teams in TVEI. There again I did a good job. I set up a system which worked well for the three years I was there, but I left because a new system was being put in its place!

Most of my other jobs fall into the category of doing a good job in a system that was fairly well established. This is true of Walsall, Birmingham and the various policy jobs I had in London: on Manpower Policy, Equal Pay and Industrial Relations and Employment of Disabled People. I was less effective as a Deputy Manager at Wolverhampton Employment Exchange and as Operations Manager in the Disablement Resettlement Service.

The least said about my spell in Maurice Macmillan's Private Office, the better! Fortunately the combined total of these three jobs was less than two years!

I am ambivalent about the value of my work in the European Commission. The work I did on work organisation was thoroughly worthwhile, but it is questionable whether we had much long-term influence on the improvement in working practices. Much of my work focused on the Working Time Directive. I was never convinced that it was a "good thing", but nor was I convinced that it was a "bad thing". As a (British) civil servant I always took the view that it was my job to set out the arguments for Ministers (and later Commissioners) for and against a policy, but, once they had taken a decision, to implement the policy in accordance with their wishes. I also considered that, when Ministers (or Commissioners) gave an undertaking in Parliament, or elsewhere, it was my job to ensure that that undertaking was honoured. In the case of the Working Time Directive, it is possible that if I had not been so assiduous in trying to find a compromise between the UK and the other delegations, the Directive may have floundered and a source of friction between the UK and Europe might have been avoided. On the other hand Labour politicians, during the unsuccessful Referendum Campaign placed some importance on retaining the right to four weeks' holiday, which was created by the Directive. It is distinctly possible that, if I had not been there, the extension of the Directive to cover 'doctors in training' might never have happened. I was possibly the only one that remembered undertakings given by the Commission in Council minutes to bring forward proposals in respect of the sectors and activities excluded from the Directive. I was the one who pointed out this commitment to Padraig Flynn. I drafted the new proposal and, drawing on my experience as Chairman of the

Social Questions Group, I was prolific in finding imaginative solutions to tricky negotiating issues.

On a personal level, my work enabled me to spend sixteen and a half years living and working abroad. For me life is always more colourful when I am abroad. I spent my 21st birthday in Switzerland and France. I said to myself then that I wanted to spend all my main birthdays abroad. Thus, I spent my 30th birthday in Swaziland and my 40th and 60th in Brussels. I have since spent my 65th, 70th and 75th birthdays in Antibes in France and my 80th in Italy. I missed out on my 50th, which I spent in Watford, but just over a year later we went back to Brussels. (I still had a good 50th birthday!) As a result of my work I visited every country in the European Union (of 15) apart from Spain. (My boss was Spanish and said I could only go in his place if I learned Spanish!) I also went to Japan in Asia; to Switzerland, Czechoslovakia, Poland, Hungary, Norway, Iceland and Cyprus in Europe; and Swaziland, South Africa, Mozambique, Zambia and Kenya in Africa. Not bad for a boring civil servant!

Skegness,
February 2021[27]

---

[27] Much of the text was written some years ago. Regrettably, some of the people that I mentioned, as being still in touch with, in particular Brian and Joan Smith and Maurice Ramond, have since passed away.

Appendix

JOINT STATEMENT

CO-OPERATION BETWEEN UNITED KINGDOM AND CZECHOSLOVAKIA IN THE LABOUR MARKET AREA

1. The British Secretary of State for Employment, Mr Michael Howard, and the Czechoslovak Federal Minister of Labour and Social Affairs, Mr Petr Miller, have agreed a programme of co-operation in the labour market area. The programme covers the following broad areas: re-training; the development of small firms; and the development of employment services. This programme will be financed under the British Government's Know-How Fund for assistance to Eastern Europe.

2. It was noted that officials from the British Employment Department had visited Czechoslovakia in March and that senior officials from the Federal Ministry of Labour and Social Affairs had spent a week in Great Britain in April. They had examined British labour market policy and the institutional framework within which it operates and in particular studied the organisation and development of the British employment service and of training arrangements.

3. Following these initial exchanges the Ministers agreed the following programme of immediate assistance:

> (a) **the establishment of arrangements for the training and re-training of adults:**
> a small team from the Federal Ministry and Czech and Slovak Ministries will visit Great Britain to study British training arrangements. The visit will begin with an intensive period of study followed by short attachments to various organisations to establish a more detailed understanding of specific aspects of training in Britain. The final stage will involve work with UK

experts to develop a 'menu' of proposals for projects to be mounted in Czechoslovakia. These projects will seek both to meet a specific local need and to demonstrate a general approach to a training problem;

(b) support to the development of small firms:
United Kingdom experts will draw up proposals in consultation with the Czechoslovakian interests for a programme of assistance for promoting and supporting the development of small firms in Czechoslovakia. Proposals will include the production and distribution of educational and training material, the promotion of enterprise among young people and the development of counselling services and local advisory agencies for those setting up businesses in Czechoslovakia;

(c) the development of employment services:
- i) a small team from the Federal Ministry and the Czech and Slovak Ministries will be sent to Great Britain to make a detailed study of the British Employment Service and services for the unemployed;
- ii) experts from the British Employment Service will provide preliminary training and advice to the senior management of the Czechoslovak employment service in the Federal Ministry of Labour and in the Czech and Slovak Ministries; this will cover corporate strategy, organisational issues and programmes of help for the unemployed including British experience in the organisation and creation of Jobclubs;
- iii) this will be followed by a training programme for employment service managers.

4. A planning group will be established to co-ordinate assistance to Czechoslovakia and to develop proposals for further assistance in the labour market area, in particular for the development of employment and training services and support for the development of small firms. The planning group will hold some meetings in Great Britain and some in Czechoslovakia. Membership of the group will include representatives of the Employment Department, the Employment Service, the Training Agency and the Joint Assistance Unit of the Foreign & Commonwealth Office in Great Britain and representatives of the Federal Ministry of Labour and Social Affairs and of the appropriate ministries in the Czech and Slovak Republics. There will be up to six people in each delegation.

5. In the longer term, officials from Czechoslovakia will study the handling of restructuring in Great Britain in particular in the coal, steel and heavy engineering industries, with regard to the re-training and re-deployment of workers. A detailed proposal will then be prepared for a project to take place in Czechoslovakia for assistance in this area.

6. The Ministers looked forward with pleasure to a beneficial and rewarding relationship between their respective ministries.

Michael HOWARD
Secretary of State
for Employment

Petr MILLER
Minister of Labour and
Social Affairs

Annex
Brexit: a Tragedy?

Tragedy: (esp. in <u>classical</u> and <u>Renaissance drama</u>) a play in which the <u>protagonist</u>, usually a <u>man of importance</u> and <u>outstanding personal</u> qualities, falls to <u>disaster</u> through the <u>combination</u> of a personal <u>failing</u> and <u>circumstances</u> with which he cannot <u>deal</u>. (Collins English Dictionary)

In this essay, I will examine the evolution of Britain's relationship with the countries of continental Europe, since the war, and seek to explore whether the vote to leave the European Union was indeed a *Tragedy*. To this end the definition above can be adapted to read: *a real life drama in which a <u>country of importance</u> and <u>outstanding national characteristics</u> and achievements falls to <u>disaster</u> through the <u>combination</u> of national failings and <u>circumstances</u> with which it cannot <u>deal</u>.*

After the war, Churchill favoured a coming together of European nations to avoid future conflicts. There is an unresolved argument as to whether he intended that Britain should be part of it. The United Kingdom (UK) took part in the discussions that led to the establishment of the European Coal and Steel Community (ECSC) in 1951, but declined to join. Throughout the fifties negotiations continued on the establishment of the European Economic Community (EEC) in 1958, of which the members were Belgium, Germany, France, Italy, Luxembourg and the Netherlands. The seeds of the Brexit tragedy were sown in that decade. As Britain took no part in the EEC negotiations, the Treaty of Rome was based on a sharing out of interests between the different founder Member States. As a gross simplification, Belgium and Luxembourg got most of the institutions, Italy got support for its poorly developed *Mezzogiorno*, Germany and the Netherlands had the benefit of a wider market for their goods, Germany footed the bill, while

France swept the board. Not only was the whole project based on a largely French legal, economic and social philosophy, but the way it was designed brought huge benefits to France's inefficient agricultural sector, as well as having the European Parliament, situated, at enormous expense, in Strasbourg. Although all four languages were equal, French was the working language. Using the Roman law of countries such as France as the basis for all EEC law is at odds with the common law in most of the English speaking world. The *Anglo-Saxon* (a French denomination) liberal, free-market economic philosophy is quite alien to traditional (i.e. 1950s) continental economic thinking. (However, one of the ironies of the present situation is that this philosophy now dominates European Union (EU) thinking, to the extent that French critics often criticise the EU for being too *Anglo-Saxon*.)

With hindsight (or even at the time), it is not surprising that Charles de Gaulle vetoed the British application to join the EEC in the sixties. He accused Britain of a "deep-seated hostility" towards European construction. Nothing (other than de Gaulle's departure) changed significantly between then and 1973, when the UK joined, accepting all the provisions of the Treaty of Rome after a transitional period.

The political arguments for the UK to join the EEC were strong then and have not altered significantly since. At the time, the economic arguments were more evenly balanced: again as a gross simplification, the choice the UK faced seemed to be between a focus on Europe or on the rest of the world, in particular the Commonwealth; it was not clear where the advantage lay. (Forty years on the economic arguments are overwhelmingly in favour of staying in the EU, but the destructive forces examined in this essay have trumped those arguments.)

An issue, which influenced the thinking of some of the Brexit campaigners, was the role of the European Court of Justice. This Court exercises considerable power and has a teleological approach to its decisions, i.e. many of the judges have considered that they have a role in the development of Community law. This, combined with the fact that it is extraordinarily difficult to repeal or limit an EU law once it has been enacted, means that there is, indeed, an acquisitive aspect, or ratchet mechanism, to the development of Community law (*l'acquis communautaire*).[1]

The issue which most soured the UK's relations with other Member States in the late seventies and early eighties was the Budget issue. As I have said earlier, under the terms of the original contract, Germany was the only net contributor (whatever their motivation was for doing so). In political circles, the French promoted the idea of solidarity between the rich and the poor and gained acceptance for the idea that a *juste retour* (fair return) was contrary to the spirit of the Treaties. However, the way the financial arrangements had been devised meant that, after a transitional period, the UK became one of only two net contributors to the EEC budget, in spite of not being one of the richest (in terms of GDP per capita). This problem was already causing concern to the Labour Government and was a major preoccupation of Margaret Thatcher throughout the eleven years (1979 to 1990) that she was Prime Minister. The £360-million-a-week figure became the main feature of the Brexit campaign.

Though it is not often mentioned, either by Brexiteers or by Europhiles in continental Europe, Margaret Thatcher was, in fact, one of the driving forces behind the creation of the Single European Market (SEM). This is the main success story of the EU and is based very largely on *Anglo-Saxon* free-market

---

[1] This means that once the EU has acquired competence in a particular area of policy, there should be no reversion to national competence.

principles. Of course, it brings with it a whole raft of detailed regulation, which is probably necessary to ensure a level playing field, but which provides ammunition for the Eurosceptics.

In 1990 under the Presidency of Jacques Delors, the Commission developed a Social Action Programme. This fuelled Euroscepticism in the UK. Michael Howard was Secretary of State for Employment. Both Michael Howard and Jacques Delors agreed with the principle of subsidiarity. Unfortunately, they had very different interpretations of what it meant in practice.

From 1991 to 2000 I worked in the unit in the Commission responsible for implementing most of the Social Action Programme and in particular the Working Time Directive. It is worth pausing for a moment to examine the differences in approach between the UK and France to industrial relations policy, or what the French call "social policy". When I joined the Ministry of Labour in 1962, apart from health and safety, there were only a few Acts of Parliament covering employment matters. The *Employment and Training Act* gave very general powers and duties to the Minister to promote employment and training.[2] The *Wages Councils Act* protected the wages and conditions of employment of workers in industries and services where trade unions were weak; there was similar legislation covering agricultural workers. The rights, such as they were, to public holidays were covered either by common law or by the *Banking and Financial Dealings* Regulations. Everything else was covered by common law or by collective agreement between

---

[2] The Minister of Labour and National Service was to provide: "Such facilities and services as he considers expedient for the purpose of assisting persons to select, fit themselves for, obtain and retain employment suitable to their age and capacity, of assisting employers to obtain suitable employees, and generally for the purpose of promoting employment in accordance with the requirements of the community." (Careers Services: History, Policy and Practice in the United Kingdom by David Peck, RoutledgeFalmer, 2004).

employers and workers or their representatives. At that time, these arrangements suited both employers' and workers' organisations. The Trades Union Congress, in particular, was opposed to Government (legislative) interference in these matters, both within the UK and within the International Labour Organisation.

The French, by contrast, had a diametrically opposite approach to these matters. The *Code de Travail* regulated everything to do with contracts of employment from minimum wages to hours of work. (The French, at least since 1936, have been obsessed with working time – hence the 35-hour week). The French have also had legislation on Works Councils, which provided the foundation for the *European Works Council Directive*.

Independently of the EU, the British Governments, over the first fifteen years of my career, began to "interfere" in employment and industrial relations matters under both Labour and Conservative governments. As well as stricter and more comprehensive laws on health and safety, there was legislation on contracts of employment, redundancy payments, industrial training, equal pay, prices and incomes, industrial relations, sex discrimination and race relations.

One might have thought that this convergence of approach would be helpful, but in fact at a detailed level, it gave rise to further conflict. For example, the phrase *where reasonably practicable,* dear to UK Health and Safety legislation, is incomprehensible to most continental lawyers.

Jacques Delors was French and the Social Action Programme was French in concept. However, the Commission's proposal for a Working Time Directive was a timid affair. Nevertheless it was sufficient to raise the wrath of Michael Howard, who was Secretary of State for Employment at the time, and, I think, a contributory factor to his growing Euroscepticism. The proposal was, however, unacceptable to the French who insisted, successfully in the course of negotiations, on the inclusion of limits on Working Time. Although the UK obtained an opt-out from these provisions, that Directive is one of the *bêtes noires* of the Eurosceptics.

The next milestone in European development was the Maastricht Treaty. This created the European Union and the euro. It is perhaps worth remembering that the French voted only narrowly in favour of the Maastricht Treaty. Had they not done so, the tragedy of Brexit might have been avoided. It was with the opt-out from the euro that the UK began to distance itself from the central European project. This set the precedent for other opt-outs, including from some aspects of the Social Action Programme. In particular, the UK opted not to sign the Schengen Agreement (not an EU agreement), which abolished (most) border controls between the signatories.

The arguments for and against joining the euro were finely balanced. I was certainly in favour. I poo-pooed the arguments of a retired British civil servant that joining the euro would inevitably lead to closer harmonisation of fiscal policy. Obviously I was wrong about that. So now there is a significant and increasing divide between those countries that are within the euro and those that are not.

The debate in the UK over the last six years, in particular, has essentially been about how much of "Europe" can we get out of or prevent from happening. Some of the reasons for that attitude are outlined above.

There are a number of other powerful forces in the UK that have undermined the British membership of the EU. Some of these are unique to the UK; some are shared by some or most other countries.

One is economic. The UK has always been an open and outward-looking economy. In particular, London is an international financial centre. A British economist in 1991 described the UK as a mid-Atlantic economy. With hindsight, it is difficult to see how the UK economy would have coped with the pressures of euro membership.

A second is cultural. While Britain's heritage is European, modern popular culture is dominated by the United States, where they speak (a sort of) English. There is also a strong influence from other English-speaking countries, particularly Australia and, increasingly, India. The pop music, film and television industries are so inextricably interconnected that I, for one, am usually hard-pressed to know whether the actors or performers are European or American. Many of the films that we watch are based in America, so that we imbibe, subconsciously, a feeling for the American way of life. Similarly, many popular novels are written by non-European authors.

A most important element is the Press. Most of the British daily newspapers are foreign-owned. As far as I know, none of these foreign owners were born in the EU. Most of them are opposed to Britain's current membership of the EU. The *Daily Mail* has for many years run stories ridiculing or trivialising the EU. The *Daily Express* campaigned successfully for a referendum. Most of the others were condescending, at best, towards the "Brussels bureaucracy". Only the *FT*, the *Guardian*, the *Independent* (and *i*) and the *Daily Mirror* were not Eurosceptic. In a similar vein, successive British Governments, in particular Conservative ones, returned from negotiations as if they were returning from a battle. *We have won concessions, we have got our money back, we have resisted Brussels' attempts to do us down* or *to waste our taxpayers' money,* etc. Unpopular legislation is portrayed as being required to comply with EU Directives. (This practice is common to most EU governments).

Next, there is immigration, which almost certainly swung the referendum in favour of Brexit. There is not room here to analyse the issue in any depth. Rightly or wrongly, immigration has been an issue in British politics at least since the early sixties. Immigrants have been blamed for many of the perceived problems in the UK: crime rates, housing problems, national identity, the National Health Service, unemployment, low wages etc. This issue is shared with many other countries and is, if anything, more acute in France than in the UK. Throughout Europe, over the last few years, there has been popular concern about immigration from outside the EU. In the UK this concern has been compounded by a large increase in immigration from within the EU. The Labour Government (and most informed commentators, including me) grossly under-estimated the numbers involved. Handled differently, this could have been seen as a windfall bonus: an influx of generally well trained and dynamic young European workers to a country with an ageing workforce and an ageing population. But insufficient measures were taken for the reception and integration of these people, who tended to gravitate towards towns, many of which were unused to large numbers of immigrants. In particular, there were problems in schools, where teachers were not trained to teach children with limited English. This problem was compounded by the Conservative manifesto promise to reduce immigration to the tens of thousands – a promise which was impossible to achieve without limits on EU migrants.

Finally, there is the referendum itself. It may be argued from the above analysis that the holding of a referendum was inevitable. But, if the Labour Party had had David Miliband as leader instead of his brother Ed, if the Liberal Democrat vote had not collapsed, there would not have been a Conservative government – though the problem might have been only postponed for another five years. In addition, the British sense of *fairness* prevailed over common sense. Normally, when there is a move to change the Constitution, the onus is on the proponents of change to make their case. With a club or association, a two-thirds majority is often required. But, in this case a simple majority was required. Furthermore, the Electoral Commission considered that a Yes/No vote was unfair and insisted on changing to Remain/Leave. Although the elected government of the UK was in favour of Remain, the BBC and ITV were bound to be neutral. Thus, whenever a Remain campaigner made a comment, the BBC was obliged to give space to a counter-argument. Furthermore, referenda are unreliable means of resolving a specific issue. I have two examples from a very small sample of people who told me they were voting or had voted to leave. One was a Green Party Councillor, who saw a leave vote as a means of getting rid of David Cameron (the British Prime Minister). The other was a retired miner, who said: "They've given us six years of austerity and then they expected us to vote for them!" Neither of these motivations had anything to do with the EU. The referendum was not binding. However, few politicians have been ready to challenge the result and there is even a debate about whether the UK Government has to consult Parliament before invoking Article 50 of the Treaty. Thus, a referendum that was partly about the sovereignty of the UK national Parliament appears to override the wishes of the members of that Parliament, who voted overwhelmingly in favour of remaining in the EU! As Enoch Powell (quoting Prometheus) said in a different context: "Those whom the gods wish to destroy, they first make mad".[3]

When looked at from the French perspective, the story looks rather different. The UK did not want to join in the first place. When it did join, it agreed to abide by the rules, but was always griping about them. Although it had agreed to the

---

[3] Enoch Powell was a senior Conservative Member of Parliament, who made a speech in 1968 criticising British immigration policy, which attracted a great deal of attention.

budgetary arrangements, it refused to comply with them, refused to accept the concept that the Community was about solidarity and banged on about "getting [their] money back". The French have often stressed the need for deepening rather than widening. The UK, on the other hand, favoured enlargement of the EU in the (mistaken) belief that it would make deepening more difficult. The French lost the argument on enlargement. In many areas of economic policy, *Anglo-Saxon* free market principles have prevailed. Agricultural policy has been reformed (though, probably, not enough) so that it is no longer as beneficial to French farmers as it was. In the labour market area, the main concern in European circles is for greater labour market flexibility, rather than protection of workers. In France criticisms of Europe are often voiced along the lines that it is too *Anglo-Saxon* or that *L'Europe Sociale* has been forgotten. Last, but by no means least, the beautiful French language has been displaced by English has the main working language in the EU.

There are strong anti-globalisation factions on both the Right and Left of French politics, which have restricted the room for manoeuvre of successive French Governments. The French are a most egocentric (or, more accurately, *national-centric*) nation. The world is seen through the French prism (perhaps even more than it is in the UK). But, whereas in the UK the knee-jerk reaction to events tends to be to distance itself from Europe, in France, paradoxically, the call is often for a deeper European involvement: Europe should be built on the French model; where it has deficiencies, it is because Europe has deviated from that model!

Of course, Europe is not just about France and the UK. Germany is now, indisputably, the most powerful force in Europe. But France has managed to forge a close bilateral relationship with Germany to the extent that most important EU meetings are preceded by a meeting between France and Germany, where, very often, they agree a common negotiating position. It could be argued that the UK has more common interests with Germany than France has: if successive British governments had played their cards differently, the UK would have had a closer relationship with Germany than France.

I may have been guilty in this essay of reinforcing the myth that the UK is the only Member State that is different from the other 27 Member States. The reality is that each Member State is different from the other 27. Some 25 years ago, I set out to demonstrate that the UK was fundamentally different from the other (eleven) Member States in relation to wages and hours of work. It was not possible to do so. On such basic issues each country has its own unique system which is based on traditions which date from long before the EEC came into being. Though I have not studied this issue in relation to other matters, it is likely to be true in many policy areas that there are widely divergent practices in each Member State.

A Tragedy?

For Brexit to be a tragedy, in the sense that I have used at the beginning of this essay - *a real life drama in which a country of importance and outstanding national characteristics and achievements falls to <u>disaster</u> through the combination of <u>national failings</u> and <u>circumstances</u> with which it cannot <u>deal</u>* – I would need to demonstrate first that the outcome was *disastrous* and then that it was indeed the result of a combination of *national failings* and *circumstances with which it cannot deal*.

It is too early to say whether the final outcome will be *disastrous*, merely economically disruptive, or, as some of the Brexiteers claim, provide the opportunity for a healthier relationship between the UK and the rest of the world.

Under the extreme tragic scenario, Brexit would fuel anti-EU and racist sentiment in other Member States, leading to the collapse of the euro and the EU. It could lead to economic protectionism and be exploited by Russia (or Donald Trump's USA[4]) to foment rivalries (and even war) between the countries of Europe. At a less extreme level, Brexit could well give rise to the break-up of the United Kingdom, a hostile relationship with the rest of Europe, a significant diminution of Britain's influence in the world and confidence in its currency, widespread unemployment and increased budgetary deficits, all of which were predicted by the Remain campaign and supported by most economists and international organisations. That, to my mind, would also be a disastrous outcome.

That element of the analysis must, however, remain unproven for the time being. It can be hoped that our drama turns out to have been not a *tragedy*, but a *farce* with a not too unhappy ending. What we can show from the above is that, if the outcome is indeed *disastrous*, the other ingredients of a potential tragedy are present: *national failings* and *circumstances with which it cannot deal*.

So what were the *national failings*? The first one was indecision: the failure in the 1950s to get fully involved in the shaping of the European project. Then, since the fall of the Heath Government in early 1974 – one year after accession – nearly all UK Governments have had an ambivalent attitude towards Europe. To this can be added the tendency of successive governments (in common with most EU governments) to portray negotiations in the EU in terms of victory or stout defence of national interests. The role of the foreign-owned popular press in the constant denigration and ridiculing of the misnamed and misunderstood *Brussels bureaucracy* has been, in my opinion, the single most important factor in the promotion of anti-EU feeling in the UK.

---

[4] This essay was written at a time when the prospect of a Trump Presidency was an alarming, but unlikely prospect!

Combined with this the British sense of *fair play* meant that the odds were stacked *against* the Government's policy: the referendum question itself; the 50/50 vote; the fact that, whereas the popular press could present one side of the argument (and lies) unchallenged, the BBC was always obliged to supply a counter-argument to every point made by the *Remain* campaign.

More important than any of that were the *circumstances with which it cannot deal*. The French have dominated the European project intellectually from the outset. Much of the philosophy is based on an idealistic notion of Europe, which often feels quite alien to most British politicians, commentators or members of the public. The notion of "ever closer union" is central to the thinking of mainstream politicians in the original core Member States, whereas most British politicians of all persuasions are uneasy with this concept. This notion led to the creation of the Single Market – the jewel in the crown, based on free-market principles. It also led to the creation of the euro and the Schengen Agreement (not strictly EU) both of which caused the UK to distance itself from the mainstream. In the present day there are many European politicians, including Martin Schulz, the President of the European Parliament, and Jean-Claude Juncker, the President of the European Commission (neither of whom is French!) for whom the notion of "ever closer union" is sacrosanct and who look upon any attempt to deviate from it as heretical or treacherous (or both!). This is the powerful force with which successive British governments have been unable to deal.

Hence the tragedy of Brexit!

Jim Mackley

August 2016

Acknowledgements

I would like to thank my son, Jon, for his help, once again, in the preparation of this book for publication.

I wish also to express my thanks to Jim Smith, who was the first to encourage me to write this book.